Hand

Dyed

Designs

I acknowledge the Boon Wurrung People of the land where I grew up and the Awabakal People of the land where I now live, and pay respect to elders past, present and emerging. Thank you for your ongoing care for the land, waters and skies.

A Guide to Dyeing Textiles with Plants

Hand
Dyed
Designs

KATIE ELLEN WILKINS

Hardie Grant

BOOKS

Contents

Introduction	6
How to use this book	8
Equipment	10

PART 1
The Basics — 14

The basics of natural dyeing	16
Mordants and modifiers	22
Dye plants	40

PART 2
Techniques — 68

Immersion-dyeing	70
Bundle-dyeing	80
Printing with leaves	96
Resist-dyeing	104
Painting with dyes and mordants	114

PART 3
Projects — 142

Avocado and onion skin silk camisole	144
Hibiscus silk shirt	147
Rust linen top	148
Indigo linen robe	150
Bleached linen jacket	154
Striped linen pants	157
Soy and cutch linen hat	158
Onion skin cotton apron	161
Madder and marigold socks	162
Handpainted linen top	165
Soy and black tea dress	166
Two-tone silk pillowcases	168
Flower-printed cotton bag	173
Ink tie-dyed silk sarong	176
Marigold velvet cushion cover	179
Cutch and iron silk top	180
Logwood sprinkled t-shirt	183
Pomegranate and geranium silk eye mask	184

PART 4
Textile Care and Sustainability — 188

Washing hand-dyed textiles	190
Spills and stains	190
Reusing a dye bath	191
Disposing of dyes and mordants	191
Sustainability	194

Glossary	198
About the Author	204
Acknowledgements	207

Introduction

I'm often asked why I'm so interested in natural dyes, and writing this book has given me an opportunity to explore answers to this question. For me, natural dyeing is the lens through which I've learnt about chemistry, history, art and botany. It has given me a unique opportunity to test my own patience, problem-solving abilities and design skills. It has forced me to look at the natural world in a new way.

I was introduced to natural dyeing after my aunt gifted me a dyeing book for my birthday and I immediately attempted it with a strong determination. I thought it would be as simple as brewing tea (and you'll come to see that *sometimes* it is), but was shocked and frustrated by the complexity of the processes. This made me even more determined to gain expertise in this intricate craft. Seven years later, I still can't quite say that I have mastered it. I still make mistakes, come up against hurdles and watch aghast as unexpected chemical reactions occur before my eyes. But I love that I will never stop learning, and that just when I feel I've got the hang of something, I might come up with a new idea that completely changes my process.

Above all, natural dyeing has taught me how much we can do with renewable resources, many of which are considered waste products. While the world is now too big to return to natural dyeing in a commercial sense, the practice itself has much to teach us about how to work with our natural world, instead of against it, and how important it is to connect with and value the textiles we use and wear. I hope that by learning how to create with natural materials and spending time connecting with nature, we will become more inclined to protect it.

While we now have synthetic dyes, which are more colourfast, easier to apply and cheaper to make, I hope this book will show that the practice of natural dyeing has relevance even in the modern age. Natural dyeing speaks to our deep desire for colour, and our reverence and perseverance in pursuing it. Applying natural colour to cloth is far from simple, and this was especially true before dye recipes had been painstakingly developed by our ancestors, and before we gained a knowledge of chemistry. Even now, most natural dyers would agree that it can be a challenging and frustrating craft, full of unexpected outcomes and subject to many variables. I think of humans thousands of years ago going through the laborious process of collecting and crushing murex snails to create Tyrian purple, despite the putrid smell produced during the dyeing process. I think of those who first discovered indigo, watching the chemical reaction as leaves soaked in a puddle mixed with the alkaline ash from a nearby fire to create the beginnings of what would be the natural source of blue. Natural dyeing exemplifies humankind's ingenuity paired with our deep love of colour and its importance for culture, self-expression and the creation of beauty.

How to use this book

This book has been written for makers and artists of all kinds, from absolute beginners to seasoned dyers. If you have never tried natural dyeing, you'll find everything you need to know here to get started from your own home. For those of you who have tried and been underwhelmed by the results, this book will clarify how to achieve the designs you're aiming for and explain why your previous experiments may not have turned out as you hoped. And for anyone who has been dyeing successfully for some time, I hope that this book will inspire you to try out some different plants or techniques and show you a few new ways of doing things.

You will find a range of information here, including very simple methods and recipes that you can make using common pantry ingredients anywhere in the world. But I have also included some more experimental and complex techniques to really challenge you in the hopes of helping you see the vast possibilities that lie in natural materials.

Every book on natural dyeing will show you a slightly different way of doing things. I have included some of the ways I like to dye, but there are countless other methods and mine are not necessarily the 'right' ones. These are the methods that work for me, and I continue to tweak certain techniques when I need to. You might find that you want to make some adjustments to my recipes, and I encourage you to do so. Natural dyeing is just like cooking – you can do it your way.

The book is divided into four parts. The first part covers the basics of natural dyeing and information on dyes and plants. I recommend that you read the section on the basics thoroughly, and you may wish to return to this and other sections as needed when you start your dyeing projects.

Part 2 covers techniques that you can use, followed by Part 3 that includes eighteen natural dyeing projects to try. This part of the book is designed much like a cookbook: each project includes a list of ingredients and instructions for how to make a particular design. I've included plenty of substitutes, so that you can use what you have on hand and can start to understand which plants make which colours. I hope you will bring your own vision and creativity to these projects by adapting the ingredients and methods to suit your own style.

The final part of the book contains information about how to care for fabrics and dispose of dyes, sustainability and a glossary of terms used in the book.

Equipment

This book includes a variety of techniques with different levels of complexity. Some will need only a bucket and hot water, for those who want to start without having to buy lots of equipment. Other techniques will require a few or all of the following:

– stainless steel pot/s* (large enough to comfortably fit your fibres)
– stainless steel strainer*
– steamer pot (such as a vegetable steamer)
– tongs and/or large spoon
– wooden dowel or plastic stick
– rubber bands
– string
– kitchen scales
– gloves
– dust mask
– paintbrushes
– glass jars
– baking paper
– steam iron
– scissors

Note on stainless steel: Natural dyes can change colour when they come in contact with metals, so we generally only use plastic or stainless steel equipment. These are non-reactive; they will not chemically react with the dye to change the colour. Metals like iron and copper can alter colour results.

PART 1

The Basics

The basics of natural dyeing

Natural dyeing involves using water and/or heat to extract the pigments from plants or insects in order to permanently dye natural fibres like silk, wool and cotton. Prior to the invention of synthetic dyes in the 1850s, all cloth was dyed using natural pigments. Usually the pigments are extracted into a pot of water called a dye bath, which can be used to achieve a variety of results. Other techniques, like bundle-dyeing, involve placing the plants directly onto the fabric before using heat to make permanent prints. It is also possible to create inks and paints and apply them to the fabric, or to use resist techniques like tie-dyeing to produce patterns. There are so many possibilities.

Regardless of which technique or project you follow from this book, there are a number of important basics that will help you understand the practice of natural dyeing. Like cooking, there are endless combinations of methods and ingredients you could use (or omit) to create a wide range of unique designs. Similarly, there are many variables that can and will affect the end result. When working with natural colour, we can't expect the same level of consistency in outcomes as we would when using a store-bought synthetic pigment. While this is a common frustration that many dyers face when trying to follow recipes or replicate designs, this is also part of the beauty of working with natural materials.

The colour you produce will depend on a number of factors. Some of these include:

- **Fabric:** Protein fibres like silk and wool have an affinity for natural dyes and will generally be easier to dye, but they will also produce different colour results. The same dye will produce a different colour depending on whether you use it on silk, wool, cotton, linen or other fibres.

- **pH:** This can be altered by adding certain ingredients (as you will discover on pages 31–39), but can also vary depending on where you are in the world. Tap water in France may be vastly different to tap water in Australia, or to rain water in Canada, and these differences can affect colour results. I'm not one to test the pH of my dye bath, but it's something that can be useful if you like to take very accurate, scientific notes.

- **Heat:** Certain dyes will change colour depending on how high the temperature is. For example, many flower dyes will lose their brightness when heated on too high a temperature, and the dye compounds found in madder root can be damaged when boiled. Other materials, like eucalyptus leaves, require high heat if you want to extract an adequate depth of colour.

- **Growing environment:** In the same way a tomato can vary widely in appearance, taste and texture, so too can dye plants and their resulting colours. Two dyes made from the same species of plant may result in different shades because of where and how they were grown and differences in nutrients, light and water.

- **Mordant:** As you will read on pages 23–31, mordants are substances that help dye adhere to fabric and prevent the colour from fading and washing out. They can also impact the end colour result: sometimes subtly, sometimes dramatically. As you begin experimenting, it will become clear to you which mordant to choose.

- **Time:** The length of time you leave your fibre in the dye will make a huge difference to the shade you can achieve. The more time it is left to soak, the deeper the shade.

Because of these variables, it's important to approach natural dyeing with an open mind and without strict expectations. There have been countless times when I've tried something new and the result has been far from what I expected. Sometimes this is a rude shock; sometimes it's a pleasant surprise. Particularly when starting out, I recommend treating everything as an experiment.

FIBRES AND FABRICS

Natural dyes work best on natural fibres: that is, fibres that have been made from either plants or animals. Plant or cellulose fibres include cotton, linen, hemp, bamboo and even more highly processed fibres like rayon, lyocell or viscose. Animal or protein fibres include wool, silk, alpaca and any other fibre made from animal hair. Plant and animal fibres need to be treated differently, and this will be covered in more detail later.

Leather can also be treated as an animal fibre when using natural dyes, while wood can be treated as a plant fibre. Although synthetic fibres may pick up some colour, they are not recommended for natural dyes as they generally don't hold the colour well.

PRE-WASHING AND SCOURING

Before dyeing or mordanting, it's important to prepare the fibres so that they are ready to take the dye. Scouring is a process that involves boiling the fibres at 90°C (195°F) for plant fibres and up to 50°C (120°F) for animal fibres, being sure to increase the temperature slowly for wool. Add 1% WOF detergent and 1% WOF sodium carbonate and soak for 30 minutes to remove any oils, waxes, gums or dirt that may prevent the dye from 'sticking'. This process can be repeated if the water post-scouring is very dirty. It is essentially a deep wash that ensures the fibres are as clean as possible and ready to absorb the mordant and pigments. Although this is highly recommended for best results, it is possible to effectively dye fibres or fabric that have simply been washed in a hot cycle in the washing machine.

PRE-WETTING

Before dyeing, dry fibres should be pre-wetted (soaked) for at least 60 minutes. This helps the fibres open up so they are ready to 'receive' the dye evenly. This is most important when your aim is to achieve an even colour, and especially with heavier fibres like cotton canvas or linen. Lightweight silks can simply be wetted under the tap prior to dyeing. If you are dyeing immediately after scouring or mordanting, your fibre will already be wet and ready to dye.

HEATING FIBRES

Some fibres require special treatment when it comes to heat. Heat is usually necessary to extract pigments from dye plants, dissolve mordants and speed up the process of both mordanting and dyeing. However, it's not essential to use heat, and I will provide multiple options for cold water mordanting and dyeing for those who would like to save energy, or don't have the necessary equipment to use on the stove.

I am not a dyer who measures the temperature of my water (I usually just take a guess), and I use the same heat for silk and plant fibres – up to 100°C (210°F) when necessary, particularly because it is difficult to bundle-dye without high temperatures. However, if you would like to be technically correct in treating your fibres with care, here are some general guidelines:

- **Plant fibres:** These are robust and can withstand high temperatures, so heating up to a boiling point of 100°C (210°F) is fine.

- **Silk:** This fibre is said to lose some of its sheen when heated, but this hasn't been my experience. If you want to be extra careful, do not heat it over 85°C (185°F). However, when bundle-dyeing, the temperature needs to reach 100°C (210°F) in order to produce steam. I have never noticed any damage to my silks from heating.

- **Wool:** This is a fibre that should be treated with care, as it can easily 'felt' and shrink when it is heated too quickly or agitated in the dye bath. Many of my wool garments have suffered this fate after accidentally ending up in a hot wash cycle. If you choose to use heat with wool for mordanting or dyeing, add the fibre to cold water and slowly increase the temperature to no higher than 90°C (195°F) so as not to 'shock' it.

MORDANTING FIBRES

The word mordant comes from the Latin *mordere* which means 'to bite'. A = mordant is a substance that helps the dye 'bite' or stick to the fibres. Without a mordant, many natural dyes would fade or wash out. It is not always essential to use a mordant and I will discuss this on pages 23–31, but it's important to remember that using a mordant will always give you the best, most colourfast results. There are numerous different mordants, and your choice will depend on the type of fibre and colour result you're after.

WEIGHING FIBRES AND DYES

The amount of dye you use in your dye bath (pot of dye) depends on how much fibre you're planning to dye. For this reason, it's advised that you weigh the dry fabric or fibre first. Most store-bought natural dyes will have a recommended quantity of dye per gram (ounce) of fibre. The terms 'weight of fibre' (WOF) and 'weight of dye' are used to measure this. For example, for dyeing with marigold I recommend using 20% WOF; so, if you have 100 grams (3.5 oz) of fibre you would use 20 grams (0.7 oz) of marigold. You can use greater or lesser quantities to achieve lighter or deeper shades. When using raw plant materials like avocado stones or eucalyptus leaves, the general rule is 100% WOF, or 100 grams (3.5 oz) of dye plant per 100 grams (3.5 oz) of fibre. It's important to remember that these are just recommendations and you'll become more confident in estimating quantities and judging by the look of the dye bath as you develop your natural dyeing skills and experience.

SAFETY

It's essential to follow some basic safety rules even when working with natural ingredients, and especially when working with mordants. These include:

– **Air flow:** Always work in a well-ventilated space. Outdoors is perfect, but a kitchen with a door or window open and a rangehood on works well too.

– **Gloves:** It's important to avoid any skin contact with mordants, so it's best to use gloves when handling fabrics that still have metal salt mordants on them (like aluminium and iron). Once the fabrics have been rinsed, it's fine to handle them with bare hands.

– **Dust mask:** A dust mask should always be worn when using fine powders like aluminium acetate to avoid inhaling particles.

– **Separate equipment:** Although it's fine to use cooking pans with dyes that are edible (like tea or onion skins), it's best to use a separate set of pots and utensils for other dyes and mordants to avoid any risk of ingesting them.

– **Children and pets:** Always keep dyes and mordants out of reach of children and pets.

– **Heat:** Always allow fabrics to cool before handling them to prevent burns.

Mordants and modifiers

Mordants are the most important ingredients to learn about when it comes to natural dyeing. They can be confusing, slightly time-consuming and involve some chemistry, but understanding how they work is essential if you want to achieve the best results. A mordant is a substance used in natural dyeing to help the dye adhere to the fabric. A mordant bonds to both the fabric and the dye, helping to fix them together permanently. Without a mordant, some dyes will wash out or fade in the sun. Other dyes can be used without a mordant (like dyes high in tannin), and produce particularly good results on protein fibres. Regardless of which dye or fabric you use, using a mordant will always improve colourfastness, and sometimes even the depth of colour.

A secondary effect of some mordants is that they can change the colour of dyes, which is called 'modifying'. Iron will 'sadden' dyes, helping to achieve shades of brown, grey, dark purple, blue and dark green which are otherwise difficult to find in natural dyes. Copper often brings out a greenish tinge in natural dyes, and tin can brighten the shade of dyes. I don't use copper or tin, but some dyers do and it's worth mentioning them, particularly when talking about colour changes. Aluminium, which is classed as a 'neutral' mordant, does not usually change the colour of natural dyes, contributing to its popularity.

It's important to weigh mordants, as per the WOF principles outlined on page 21. Failure to do so can have a significant impact on the end result. For example, if you use too much iron, the fibres can weaken; if you use too much aluminium, you may end up having to pour it down the drain. If you don't use enough of any mordant, you may end up with poorer results. When using mordants, it's also important to make sure that there is enough water in the pot for the fabric to move around freely. This will ensure that the result is even and not patchy.

Regardless of which resource you use to learn about mordanting, you will find slight variations in methods. The aim here is to give you a few simple yet effective methods, rather than overloading you with options and confusing chemistry.

PLANT-BASED MORDANTS

Tannin

Tannins are naturally occurring molecules found in bark, wood, leaves, roots, fruits, seeds and plant galls. Tannins are commonly used for tanning leather to make it more durable; in winemaking to change the taste and texture; in photography during the development process; for some medical treatments; and also as effective mordants for plant fibres in natural dyeing.

You can use tannin on its own as a mordant for plant fibres like cotton or linen, or use it prior to mordanting with aluminium, which is what I would recommend for best results. You can find tannin in many dye plants such as avocado stones, pomegranate rinds or acorns, or you can buy it as a powdered dye extract which is usually made from oak bark and leaves. Some tannins are clear and don't colour the fabric, and some will dye it light shades of brown or yellow. Tannin can be a good option for those who prefer not to use metal salts like aluminium or iron.

- **Quantity:** Use powdered tannin (tannic acid) at 8% WOF on plant fibres. When using a raw dye plant, use equal quantities of dye and fibre (e.g., 100 grams [3.5 oz] plant for 100 grams [3.5 oz] fibre).

- **Instructions for tannin powder:** Dissolve 8% WOF tannin powder in warm water and add to the pot. Add the pre-wetted fibre and slowly increase the heat and allow to simmer for about 60 minutes, stirring occasionally. An alternative is to switch off the heat when you immerse the fibre and allow it to soak with the lid on for 1–2 hours. You can then rinse the fibre and dye immediately or follow with aluminium. Alternatively, you can rinse, dry and store the fabric to dye later.

- **Instructions for tannin from a raw plant:** Add 100% WOF of a plant high in tannin to a pot of water. Allow to simmer for around 60 minutes to extract the tannin. Remove the pot from the heat, strain the plant material from the dyeing liquid, add the pre-wetted fibre to the pot and put a lid on the pot. Allow it to soak for 1–2 hours, then proceed to dye. Alternatively, you can rinse, dry and store the fabric to dye later.

- **Plants high in tannin include:** avocado stones, acorns, oak galls/bark, eucalyptus leaves, cutch, fustic, quebracho, black walnut, myrobalan, pomegranate rind, tara, black tea, coffee and chestnut.

Soy

Soy milk is not technically a mordant; rather, it's a 'binder'. Animal fibres contain proteins that have an affinity for natural dyes, whereas soy contains proteins that help plant fibres act more like animal fibres and consequently give better results. By using soy milk as a binder on plant fibres, colours can be deeper and more colourfast. Although it is not as commonly used as aluminium, soy milk is incredibly effective and I would highly recommend it for anyone who wants to dye plant fibres without having to purchase a mordant.

THE BASICS

- **Quantity:** Use store-bought soy milk without any additives or oils, or make your own using soy beans and water. Dilute the soy milk with cold water at a ratio of 1:5.
- **Instructions:** Once the soy milk has been diluted, add the pre-wetted plant fibre, making sure it has plenty of room to move freely. Allow it to soak for around 12 hours, then rinse gently in cold water. Allow the fibre to dry completely, then proceed to dye or store for later use.

> **Tip:** It can be beneficial to allow soy-treated fibres which have dried completely to 'cure' by letting them sit for a few weeks before dyeing. This is not essential but can help you achieve deeper shades if you have the time.

Top (left to right): Madder root on cotton with no mordant, soy milk binder, aluminium, iron.

Middle (left to right): Cutch on cotton with no mordant, soy milk binder, aluminium, iron.

Bottom (left to right): Black tea on silk with no mordant, aluminium, iron.

MINERAL MORDANTS

Aluminium sulphate and aluminium potassium sulphate

Aluminium sulphate and aluminium potassium sulphate produce near identical results. Aluminium sulphate comes in larger granules that look similar to rock salt. Aluminium potassium sulphate comes in smaller granules, similar to white sugar, and is slightly more costly. Aluminium is commonly used for water purification, to regulate soil pH, in cosmetics, in the pharmaceutical industry and in food production. It is also a widely used mordant in natural dyeing and is valued for its low toxicity (considered non-hazardous), affordability and neutrality, meaning it won't change the colour of the dye. Both aluminium sulphate and aluminum potassium sulphate can be used to mordant protein fibres and in combination with tannin to mordant plant fibres.

– **Quantity**: Use aluminium sulphate or aluminium potassium sulphate at 10%–15% WOF for best results.

– **Instructions**: Measure and place aluminium sulphate or aluminium potassium sulphate in a vessel with enough hot water (90°C [195°F]) to dissolve the granules. Fill a pot with room temperature water and pour in the dissolved mordant. Immerse your scoured, pre-wetted fibres in the mordant solution. Bring the water up to 90°C (195°F). At this point you can leave the heat on a simmer for around 60 minutes, or turn off the heat and place a lid on to keep the heat in for around 2 hours. Remove the fibre and rinse it. Either dye it immediately or dry and store it for later use.

Opposite, top to bottom: Aluminium sulphate, aluminium potassium sulphate, aluminium acetate, ferrous sulphate, tannin.

Aluminium acetate

Aluminium acetate is my choice for mordanting plant fibres. It is an alternative to aluminium sulphate and aluminium potassium sulphate and is slightly more expensive, but gives the best results and allows you to skip the tannin step. Aluminium acetate also works on protein fibres, but the less costly aluminium potassium sulphate is just as effective.

- **Quantity:** Use aluminium acetate at 5%–8% WOF.
- **Instructions:** Dissolve the aluminium acetate in a pot of hot water from the tap (50°C [120°F]). Add the fibre and allow it to soak for 1–2 hours, stirring occasionally. Remove the fibre and soak it in a bath of hot tap water with 5% WOF calcium carbonate or 5% WOF wheat bran for 10–30 minutes. Either dye it immediately, or dry and store it for later. It is also possible to use cold water with aluminium acetate.

Iron (ferrous sulphate)

Iron, or ferrous sulphate, is a mineral mordant that can be used either before or after dyeing on plant or protein fibres. When used before dyeing, it is a reliable mordant that also changes the colour of dyes, making it possible to achieve deep greens, blues, browns, greys and even blacks. When used as a modifier after dyeing, iron will still change the colour of dyes, but using it before dyeing improves colourfastness as well.

- **Quantity:** Iron should be used at around 1%–2% WOF. Using too much iron can make fibres brittle and prone to breakage.
- **Instructions:** Dissolve iron in a pot of hot water from the tap (50°C [120°F]). Add the fibre and allow it to soak for roughly 10 minutes for animal fibres and a maximum of 30 minutes for plant fibres. Leaving the fabric in iron for too long can weaken its fibres and/or produce orange stains where the iron has oxidised. Always rinse the fibres in cold water after mordanting to remove any iron that has not bonded to the fibre.

Copper, chrome and tin

Historically, chrome and tin were commonly used in natural dyeing, but it's now known that they are toxic so using iron or aluminium is safer. Copper is still used by some dyers, but I only use aluminium and iron.

COLD MORDANTING

Although most dyers use hot water, you can use cold water to save energy and to dye without needing a stove. It will require more time for the mordanting process, which means that instead of leaving the fabric in a hot water mordant for 1–2 hours, you can leave it in a cold water mordant for 1–3 days. My choice is to use hot water from the kettle to dissolve the mordant, then allow my fibres to soak for 1–2 hours with a lid on. This is effective and also reduces energy use.

ALL-IN-ONE

It's possible to add the mordant directly to the dye bath, skipping the pre-mordant process. The downside is that it can cause the dye and mordant to bond in the water, rather than on the fabric, forming a sludge at the bottom of the dye bath. It is always more effective to pre-mordant the fabric, rinse off any excess mordant, then add the fibre to the dye bath.

MAKING YOUR OWN MORDANT

Pot as mordant

Although we generally use stainless steel pots for dyeing, it's possible to use an aluminium, copper or iron pot for a two-in-one process where the metal in the pot itself acts as a mordant. This has some benefits, including reducing time, materials and energy. However, only a limited amount of metal will leech into the water, so it will never be as effective as using a mordant in powdered form. It is also impossible to measure the mordant for your weight of fibre when using this method. In order to use a pot as a mordant, simply replace a stainless steel pot with one made from aluminium, copper, tin or iron. This method is most effective as a modifier.

DIY mordant

If you don't have access to iron salts, it is possible to make your own at home. However, in the same way that using a pot as a mordant won't be as effective as traditional mordanting, your home-made mordant may not produce a reliable level of colourfastness. As it's virtually impossible to measure the amount of metal that ends up in the mordant in comparison to the weight of fibre you are dyeing, you may find that you have too little or too much for the fibre. Don't let this deter you though, as it can still be very effective. Just ensure you test the mordant on a small piece of fabric before dyeing larger items to avoid unwanted colour changes.

- **Quantity:** Use a 500 ml (17 fl oz) jar and a rough handful of rusty nails, iron or copper.
- **Instructions:** Soak the rusty nails in the jar in a solution of vinegar and water in a 1:1 ratio for 2 weeks. Once the colour of the vinegar water changes to orange, the mordant is ready for use. Add the jar of mordant to a pot filled with warm water and immerse the fibres. Allow them to soak for 10–30 minutes. Remove the fibre and either dye immediately or dry it for later use.

USING NO MORDANT

Although using a mordant is the best way to ensure colourfastness and the longevity of your textiles, it is not always essential. There are a couple of exceptions to using a mordant. Dyes high in tannin are very effective on protein fibres without a mordant. I have dyed many silk pillowcases using cutch without a mordant and have seen no fading over the course of five years. I even wash these in a regular cycle in a washing machine. This is a good option for beginners, as sometimes mordanting can feel overwhelming at the start. Dyes high in tannin are very effective on protein fibres without a mordant.

Some mordant options

Plant fibres

- **Aluminium acetate at 5%–8% WOF:** Best as a neutral mordant that is effective and doesn't require pre-mordanting with tannin. Follow with a calcium carbonate afterbath for 10–30 minutes. I have also had good results without the calcium carbonate afterbath.

- **Iron at 1%–2% WOF:** Best to create darker shades of grey, dark blue, brown, purple, dark green and even black.

- **Soy binder diluted 1:5:** Best for those who don't want to use a metal salt like iron or aluminium. Very effective when used in combination with dyes high in tannin.

- **Tannic acid at 8% WOF (or raw plant tannin at 100% WOF):** Best for those who don't have access to soy or a metal salt, or those who have a dye that is already high in tannin and want to skip the mordanting process (since the dye contains the mordant in this case).

- **Tannic acid at 8% WOF (or raw plant tannin at 100% WOF) followed by aluminium potassium sulphate or aluminium sulphate at 10% WOF**: Best for those who don't have access to aluminium acetate but want to ensure optimal colourfastness. This process is a little more time-consuming.

Protein fibres

- **Aluminium potassium sulphate or aluminium sulphate at 10%–15% WOF:** Best as a neutral mordant that will provide excellent colour- and lightfastness with most types of dye.

- **Iron at 1%–2% WOF:** Best for those looking to create darker shades of grey, dark blue, brown, purple, dark green and even black.

- **No mordant when using a dye high in tannin:** Best for those who have a dye high in tannin and want to skip the mordanting step.

ASSISTS AND MODIFIERS

The term 'assist' is used to describe an optional ingredient that you can add to mordants to improve results. These can be used to alter the fibres: for example, to soften wool. The same ingredients can also be called 'modifiers', depending on when they are used in the dyeing process and for what purpose. Modifiers are often used to change the pH level of a dye, which alters the colour. As many natural dyes are pH-sensitive, they can dramatically change colour when an alkali or acid is added. Many new dyers mistake assists and modifiers for mordants, but these substances do not prevent dyes from fading or washing out. Rather, they can be used as post-mordant fixatives, fabric cleaners or softeners, or to modify colours.

Alkalis

Alkaline modifiers will generally change browns to reds, reds to darker reds, yellows to oranges, and purples to blues or greens.

- **Sodium carbonate:** Also known as soda ash or washing soda, sodium carbonate is commonly used during scouring to remove oil and dirt from fibres. It is an alkali that can also be used in a dye bath to increase the pH and consequently create colour changes.

- **Sodium bicarbonate:** Also known as bicarbonate of soda (baking soda) or shortened to bicarb soda, sodium bicarbonate is an alkali. It is not as strong as sodium carbonate and will create a less dramatic colour change. However, it is still very useful in natural dyeing and can be used to raise the pH.

- **Calcium carbonate:** Also known as chalk, calcium carbonate has a pH of around 8–11, making it quite alkaline. It is commonly used in madder dye baths to deepen the red shade since madder loves 'hard' water. It can also be used after mordanting with aluminium acetate to fix the mordant.

THE BASICS

Opposite, top (left to right): Cutch on silk with no modifier, acidic modifier, alkaline modifier, iron.

Opposite, bottom (left to right): Hibiscus on silk with no modifier, acidic modifier, alkaline modifier, iron.

Red geraniums on paper with sodium carbonate water and lemon juice modifiers.

Acids

Acidic modifiers used in small amounts will generally lighten and brighten colours. Some strong acidic modifiers can act as bleaching agents by removing mordants in fibres (see page 154).

- **Vinegar:** Slightly acidic and commonly used during bundle-dyeing to brighten colours, white vinegar can be used in a spray bottle and sprayed over the fabric.

- **Cream of tartar:** Often used in combination with aluminium to mordant wool, cream of tartar can help to soften fibres. It has a pH of around 3–4, making it acidic, so it can also be used to change or brighten colours when added to a dye bath.

- **Citric acid:** This can be purchased in powder form or obtained from lemon juice. I have often used lemon juice to create a bleached effect. Citric acid can damage the bond between the mordant and fibre (also known as discharging), so it's not recommended unless you want to strip away colour.

Metal salts

Metals and metal salts are generally used as mordants, but they can also be used to change the colour of natural dyes.

- **Iron:** Also known as ferrous sulphate, will 'sadden' dyes, turning colours to dark browns, blues, greys, greens and even blacks.

- **Copper:** Use of copper can have the effect of shifting colours to a greener tone. It can be purchased from a natural dye supply store, although I personally do not use it.

- **Aluminium:** Considered to be a neutral mordant, aluminium does not dramatically change the colour of dyes in the same way that other metal salts do, but it does tend to brighten and deepen shades.

HOW TO MODIFY A COLOUR

One of the best things about natural dyeing is that if you don't like what you've dyed, there are many ways you can change it. You can redye it completely by bundle-dyeing your fabric again with different plants or immersing it in a new dye bath. You can paint over it, or you can change the colour using a modifier. Modifying a colour involves using an acid or alkali to change the pH, consequently changing the colour of the dye and fabric. Metal salts like iron and copper can also be used to change the colour of dyes. Once you know how modifiers work, you can choose to apply them before, during or after dyeing.

Adding a modifier to a dye bath

An easy way to change the colour of a dye is by adding the modifier directly to the dye bath itself. To do this, add a small amount of one of the modifiers listed below to your dye bath until the colour changes to your liking. Here are some suggestions of quantities to start with:

- **Sodium carbonate:** Add 1% WOF to 100 ml (3.4 fl oz) hot water and stir until completely dissolved. Pour the solution into the dye bath and wait at least 2 minutes before testing with a fabric scrap. Increase at this quantity each time if necessary, waiting for a couple of minutes before adding more.

- **Sodium bicarbonate:** Add 2% WOF to 100 ml (3.4 fl oz) hot water and stir until completely dissolved. Pour the solution into the dye bath and wait at least 2 minutes before testing with a fabric scrap. Increase at this quantity each time if necessary, waiting for a couple of minutes before adding more.

- **Vinegar:** Add white vinegar at 5% WOF directly to the dye bath, stir and wait for at least 2 minutes before testing with a fabric scrap. Increase at this quantity each time if necessary, waiting for a couple of minutes before adding more.

- **Iron (ferrous sulphate):** Dissolve iron powder at 1% WOF in a jar of hot or boiling water and stir until completely dissolved. Pour half the jar into the dye bath, stir and wait for 2 minutes. Test with a piece of scrap fabric and pour in the rest of the jar if you want to continue darkening the shade. Repeat until the desired shade is reached. Do not use more than 2% WOF, as this will weaken the fibres.

- **Rusty objects:** Rather than making an iron mordant using rusty objects, you can just add them directly to the dye bath. Since it is difficult to measure the iron in rusty objects, simply add a few pieces of iron to the dye bath and see what happens over about 15 minutes. Add more if necessary and remove them when you reach your desired shade.

- **Cream of tartar:** Add 5% WOF to a jar of hot or boiling water and stir until completely dissolved. Pour the entire jar into the dye bath and wait at least 2 minutes before testing with a fabric scrap. Increase at this quantity each time if necessary, waiting for a couple of minutes before adding more.

Opposite: Avocado dyed silk modified with (left to right) iron, acidic and alkaline water.

- **Citric acid:** Add 5% WOF (or roughly 50 ml [1.7 fl oz] lemon juice) to a jar of hot water and stir until completely dissolved. Pour the entire jar into the dye bath and wait at least 2 minutes before testing with a fabric scrap. Increase at this quantity each time if necessary, waiting for a couple of minutes before adding more.

Modifier dip post-dyeing

Dipping pre-dyed fabric in a modifier solution is one of the easiest ways to change a design you don't like. It also gives you more control over the colour result, as you can remove it as soon as it reaches your desired colour. The method for each modifier is the same; the difference is in the WOF.

Quantity:

- Sodium carbonate: 1% WOF

- Sodium bicarbonate: 2% WOF

- Vinegar: 5% WOF

- Iron: 1% WOF

- Cream of tartar: 5% WOF

- Citric acid: 5% WOF or 50 ml (1.7 fl oz) lemon juice

    Instructions: Fill a stainless steel pot or plastic bucket with hot tap water. The water will be around 50°C (120°F). You can heat the water up to 90°C (195°F). Add your chosen modifier in the quantity listed above. Stir until the modifier is completely dissolved. Add the pre-dyed, wet fibre to the dye bath, stirring until you see a colour change. Remove the fibre or add more of your chosen modifier until you achieve the desired shade. Remove the fibre from the pot and rinse in cold water using a gentle detergent.

Discharging a mordant

The term 'discharge' is used in natural dyeing to describe the process of using citric acid to remove or discharge the effect of a metal mordant (like iron or aluminium) to part of the fabric in order to create contrast. The citric acid damages the bond between the mordant and the fibre, and acts similarly to bleach by stripping the colour away. In the area where the acid has been applied, the mordant is no longer effective and instead there is a lighter contrast. This process is particularly effective when discharging an iron mordant. The image opposite shows cotton mordanted with iron, dyed with tannin and then discharged with lemon juice.

Dye plants

There are countless plants that can be used for dyeing, and while I have selected some of my favourites here, don't be afraid to try other plants in your area. The worst that can happen is that they don't work; the best that can happen is that you find a beautiful new colour. I've chosen the following plants for a number of reasons, but the most important is that they are tried and tested. Many of the plants listed here are traditional dye plants that have been used for thousands of years, so you can be sure that they will give you vibrant results. I've also included a number of plants that are found in your kitchen or garden regardless of where you live, and plenty that can be purchased online. As you read through this section, you'll notice that each plant is unique and some have particular needs in order to produce the best shades. As always, experimentation is the best teacher, and you will begin to understand through practice how to treat each dye plant.

STORING DYE PLANTS

My general rule is that fresh is best, but you can get excellent results from dried plants too. Sometimes you might collect dye plants that you don't have time to use right away, in which case you can freeze or dry them. Dried or frozen plants will produce different colours to fresh plants. The colour from geraniums, for example, will 'bleed' when they're fresh, which means that if you use them for bundle-dyeing, you'll notice the colour spreads more. It's fun to see what different results you can get by changing up the way you prepare your plants.

Freezing

Freezing is the best way to get results that are similar to using plants fresh. It is also particularly useful for plant matter like avocado stones, which may grow mould and begin decomposing if left to dry. I store these kinds of plants in a plastic zip-lock bag or reusable container. This is also a great way to store flowers or other kitchen items like red cabbage that wouldn't dry easily.

Drying

Dried plants often provide a different colour and pattern result to fresh plants. If you want to dry dye plants, make sure you lay them out flat and give them plenty of air so they don't get mouldy. If you're working with petals or small leaves, you can lay them on a baking tray in the sun or in a dry cupboard. Larger pieces and bunches of flowers or branches can be pegged to the washing line. Once they are completely dry, they can be stored in a jar or flat in a book. Things like onion skins that are already dry can be stored in a jar immediately. Drying works well with most flowers, leaves, roots, bark, wood and nuts, but not so well with fruit or vegetables.

DYE PLANTS TO TRY

Avocado (*Persea americana*)

Avocado skins and stones are excellent dye sources for first-timers. They are easy to source, cheap (since they are a food by-product) and high in tannin, which means they can achieve colourfast results on both plant and protein fibres. I recommend using soy as a mordant for avocado stones with plant fibres, and using no mordant for protein fibres. You can achieve a range of shades of pink, blush and salmon depending on your chosen fabric. The stones will generally result in a deeper pink colour than the skins, which are often more of a light orange or salmon, or you can use the stones and skins together.

- **Colours:** Pale pink, coral, salmon, silver, dark grey.

- **Colourfastness:** Stones – excellent; skins – moderate.

- **Dyeing:** Skins or stones – 100% WOF.

- **Heat:** Avocado stones will produce a muddy brown unless heated low and slow. Bring the dye bath to around 85°C (185°F) or just below a simmer. Hold the water at this temperature for at least 1 hour and up to 3 hours, or until the water is a bright, deep pink.

- **Storage:** Wash off all the flesh and freeze. Drying is also possible, and if mould appears, wash it off.

- **Options:** Avocado stones can be used in any dyeing technique other than bundle-dyeing. However, it is possible to use avocado *skins* for bundle-dyeing.

THE BASICS

Black walnut (*Juglans nigra*)

Native to North America, walnut hulls (also known as husks) have been used for centuries to make inks, hair dyes, textile dyes and for medicinal purposes. They make a very strong, tannin-rich dye, which provides reliable shades of brown and black even without a mordant (but as always, a mordant provides the best result). The green husks can be heated whole to create a rich dye bath, or used dried or frozen. If the husks are old or no longer green, they can still produce a successful dye. It's not necessary to remove the nut, but you can, and it's recommended that you strain walnut dyes to remove sediments.

- **Colours:** Tan, light brown, dark brown, almost black.
- **Colourfastness:** Excellent.
- **Dyeing:** Powder – 20%–100% WOF; raw plant – 50%–100% WOF.
- **Heat:** It's necessary to use high heat, around 90°C–100°C (195°F–210°F) to extract the pigment from walnut hulls. Hold the water at this temperature for at least 60 minutes for best results.
- **Storage:** Dry or freeze. Black walnut hulls can be dried and stored in an airtight jar indefinitely.
- **Options:** Black walnut hulls can be used in any dyeing technique other than bundle-dyeing. They can also be used as a mordant for plant fibres due to their high tannin content. They are excellent for making paints and inks for both fabric and paper.

Madder (*Rubia tinctorum* or *Rubia cordifolia*)

The use of madder root as a natural dye can be dated back to at least 2000 BCE, and remnants of madder-dyed textiles have been found preserved in tombs, including that of the Egyptian pharaoh Tutankhamun. Madder roots are left to grow for up to five years before harvesting to ensure the highest level of alizarin, the dye compound used to make shades of red. They are then dried and ground or left whole and used in combination with hot water to make a red dye. Over time, madder came to be regarded alongside indigo as one of the best natural dye sources, but it fell out of popular use when red dyes were synthesised in the late 1800s. Madder develops the deepest reds in hard water and for this reason it is often recommended to add a small amount of an alkaline modifier such as sodium carbonate to the dye bath. You can grow madder plants from seed at home.

- **Colours:** Scarlet, Turkey red, brick red, wine red.
- **Colourfastness:** When mordanted properly, madder-dyed fabric has excellent colourfastness. Without a mordant it can fade or wash out.
- **Dyeing:** Roots – 100% WOF; extract – 5% WOF; powder – 20%–30% WOF.
- **Heat:** If madder is overheated it will turn brown and muddy. Bring a pot of water up to 80°C (175°F) for roughly 60 minutes (raw roots) or 20 minutes (extracts/powders).
- **Storage:** Powder, extract and raw roots should be kept in an airtight container.
- **Options:** Add sodium carbonate at 5% weight of dye to the dye bath for a deeper red. Using an acidic modifier like cream of tartar or vinegar will produce more orange shades. When used with an iron mordant or modifier, colours will shift to a dark red to deep purple/brown.

Oak (*Quercus* species)

If you have an oak tree nearby, you have immediate access to one of the most versatile and hardy plants to use for mordanting and dyeing. With over 400 species, oaks have been around for about 56 million years, and are commonly found throughout the northern hemisphere. Many parts of the plant can be used for dyeing, including acorns, leaves, bark and gallnuts. Gallnuts are a hard ball that forms when a gall insect lays its larvae on the tree. The tree releases a secretion as a defence mechanism and this tannin-rich gum forms into a 'nut', which has been used for tanning and ink-making purposes for centuries. Gallnuts are commonly used as a mordant for plant fibres due to their high tannin content, but acorns, bark and leaves can also be used. Oak species are particularly good for achieving a near black dye, which is rare in natural dyeing. If you don't have an oak tree near you, you can purchase gallnut powder or tannic acid for use as a mordant or dye. Oak galls contain a clear tannin, meaning they barely produce any colour without iron. You can use any part of the oak tree as a tannin mordant.

- **Colours:** Tan, light brown, purple/blue.
- **Colourfastness:** Excellent.
- **Dyeing:** Acorns, bark, gallnuts, leaves – 100% WOF; extract – 8% WOF.
- **Heat:** It's usually necessary to use a high heat of 90°C–100°C (195°F–210°F) to extract the pigment from acorns, bark and gallnuts. Hold the water at this temperature for at least 60 minutes for best results.
- **Storage:** All parts of the plant can be dried and stored in an airtight jar indefinitely.
- **Options:** Oak is excellent for making near black paint and inks for both fabric and paper when mixed with iron. The leaves work well for bundle-dyeing.

Cutch (*Acacia catechu*)

Cutch is a natural extract made from the heartwood of an acacia tree native to South and South-East Asia. Since it is an extract, not a powder, it dissolves almost completely in water, making it an excellent option for inks and paints. Cutch is a beautiful dye to use for its range of shades. The dye bath can take a long time to exhaust, meaning that it can be reused again and again to achieve lighter shades. Cutch is high in tannin, which is perfect for beginner dyers who may like to start slow without mordanting on protein fibres. It can be purchased in extract form.

- **Colours:** Tan, light brown, rust, light pink, dark brown.

- **Colourfastness:** Excellent.

- **Dyeing:** Extract – 20%–30% WOF.

- **Heat:** Cutch will produce a good dye bath in cold, warm or hot baths. If using cold water, dissolve the extract in a small amount of boiling water before adding cutch to a cold bath. I recommend using water that is just below boiling.

- **Storage:** Store in an airtight container.

- **Options:** Dark brown when used with iron, and a lovely red-brown (20%–30% WOF) or light pink (10% WOF or less) when used with an alkali like sodium carbonate. Cutch can be used for any dyeing technique but since it is an extract, it should be used carefully and frugally when bundle-dyeing to avoid big, dark brown blotches.

THE BASICS

Fustic (*Chlorophora tinctoria*)

Fustic is a potent dye extract that is obtained from the heartwood of a species of tree native to Central and South America. It is one of the most colourfast sources of yellow due to its high tannin content, and was used during the First World War to dye khaki uniforms for soldiers. Today it can be purchased online, although it is costly. When mixed with indigo, fustic can produce teal and forest greens, which are rare among natural dyes. Although it is expensive, you only need to use a small amount, so a little goes a long way.

- **Colours:** Yellow, orange, grey/green.
- **Colourfastness:** Excellent.
- **Dyeing:** Extract – 2%–5% WOF.
- **Heat:** Fustic will produce a good dye bath in cold, warm or hot water. If using cold water, dissolve the extract in a small amount of boiling water before adding it to a cold bath. I recommend using water that is just below boiling.
- **Storage:** Store in an airtight container.
- **Options:** When using fustic for bundle-dyeing, be mindful that the dye is very strong and can be overpowering.

Logwood (*Haematoxylum campechianum*)

Native to Mexico, logwood is a favourite dye plant due to its ability to create blues and purples. This is relatively rare among natural dyes, which tend to produce more yellows, oranges, reds and browns. Logwood can be expensive, but it makes some incredible colours, from purples to pale baby blue. It can be purchased as woodchips or extract.

- **Colours:** Purple, blue, dark blue.
- **Colourfastness:** Moderate. Logwood requires a mordant on plant or protein fibres. When used with an aluminium mordant, the bright purple can fade over time. However, when used with an iron mordant, logwood holds its deep, dark blues extremely well.
- **Dyeing:** Extract – 1%–2% WOF; woodchips – 10%–15% WOF.
- **Heat:** Logwood chips can be simmered for about 45 minutes in order to extract the pigment for immersion-dyeing. Logwood extract will also dissolve into cold water if hot water is not available.
- **Storage:** Store extract or woodchips in an airtight container.
- **Options:** Bundle-dyeing with logwood chips can create some really unique patterns. The chips can be kept and reused, as they often retain a lot of pigment. Bundle-dyeing with logwood extract can also create a beautiful speckled pattern.

Marigold (*Tagetes*)

Marigolds can flower from spring to autumn and are valued in dyeing all over the world for their beautiful shades of orange and yellow. Native to Mexico, marigolds were brought to India in the sixteenth century and are now an important part of festivities and cultural celebrations. One of the easier dye plants to grow at home, marigolds grow best in well-drained soil in part or full sun. They are available in a variety of colours, including yellow, orange and red. Marigolds can be used dry, fresh or as a powder.

- **Colours:** Orange, yellow, olive green.
- **Colourfastness:** Moderate. A mordant should be used for best results.
- **Dyeing:** Powder – 20%–30% WOF; flowers – 100% WOF.
- **Heat:** Use hot water at around 90°C (195°F) for best results and hold the water at this temperature for roughly 30 minutes before immersing fibres.
- **Storage:** Flowers can be dried or frozen. Powder can be stored in an airtight container.
- **Options:** Perfect for immersion-dyeing or bundle-dyeing.

Osage orange (*Maclura pomifera*)

Native to Central United States, Osage orange is a small deciduous tree that produces a green, lumpy, inedible fruit the size of a softball. Native Americans, including the Osage people that it's named after, used the wood for making archery bows due to its strength and flexibility. Later it became popular for building fences and was dubbed *bois d'arc* (bow-wood) by French explorers. It was also used to dye khaki uniforms during the First World War. The sawdust made from the Osage orange tree makes gorgeous yellows and oranges, as well as mossy greens with iron.

- **Colours:** Yellow, orange, olive green.
- **Colourfastness:** Moderate. As long as a mordant is used, Osage orange will also provide good light- and washfastness.
- **Dyeing:** Woodchips or sawdust – 20%–30% WOF.
- **Heat:** Osage orange requires boiling water for at least 60 minutes to extract the pigment from the sawdust or woodchips.
- **Storage:** The sawdust should be stored in an airtight container.
- **Options:** Any woodchips used when bundle-dyeing may pierce the fabric, so care is needed.

THE BASICS

Safflower (*Carthamus tinctorius*)

Safflower petals have been used for centuries to dye textiles and for cosmetics. Safflower oil is made from the seeds and is commonly used in cooking. This magical plant can produce both bright yellow and pink dyes depending on how the colour is extracted. Safflower can be purchased in dried form.

- **Colours:** Yellow, pink, olive green.
- **Colourfastness:** Low to moderate.
- **Dyeing:** Dried petals – 100% WOF.
- **Heat:** Safflower dye can be made without heat. The red dye appears after multiple soakings. By soaking the petals at room temperature, a yellow dye will be released. Once the yellow dye has been exhausted, the yellow dye can be set aside and the petals resoaked. An alkaline modifier like sodium carbonate can be used to shift the pH to 11 and the petals soaked for 60 minutes. Removing the petals and using an acid to shift the pH back to 6 will result in a bright pink dye.
- **Storage:** Store dried petals in an airtight container.

Hibiscus (*Hibiscus rosa-sinensis*)

Native to China, the *Hibiscus rosa-sinensis* has been used throughout history for various health purposes due to its antioxidant, anti-inflammatory and antimicrobial properties. Now approximately 200 species of hibiscus can be found worldwide. Although the hibiscus is not a traditional natural dye for fabric, it has been found to contain both tannin and flavonoids, which are important chemicals found in many dye plants. I highly recommend this beautiful plant for its ability to create purples and blues, which are rare in natural dyes. Hibiscus flowers or tea can be used for dyeing but sometimes they are mixed with other plants that are less useful for dyeing, so it is worth checking ingredients. Only use the deep pink and red flowers.

- **Colours:** Purple, blue, dark blue.

- **Colourfastness:** Low to moderate. The use of iron will increase colourfastness.

- **Dyeing:** 100% WOF.

- **Heat:** It is recommended to use heat for dyeing with hibiscus flowers. Heat them in a pot of water at 80°C (175°F) for around 30 minutes to create a dye bath.

- **Storage:** Hibiscus flowers can be dried individually or frozen for later use.

- **Options:** Fresh hibiscus petals work well for bundle-dyeing. Try also using rose species, which create various shades of pink, purple and blue.

Eucalyptus species

With over 900 species, this Australian native is one of the strongest sources of natural dye. High amounts of tannin are contained in the leaves and bark, and eucalyptus dyes are not only colourfast but can also produce a wide variety of shades, from yellow, orange, pink, and red to brown, grey and dark blue when used with iron. Eucalyptus leaves are commonly used to create crisp, clear, leaf-shaped prints on all fibres, and gum blossoms can also be used to create unique prints when bundle-dyeing. While most eucalyptus leaves produce a yellow/orange with a neutral mordant or a dark grey/blue with iron, certain species like the silver dollar eucalyptus can produce bright pinks or reds on protein fibres. It's important to work in a well-ventilated area when boiling eucalyptus leaves, as the fumes can be quite strong.

- **Colours:** Red, brown, yellow, orange, pink, grey, dark blue.
- **Colourfastness:** Excellent.
- **Dyeing:** Leaves – 100% WOF.
- **Heat:** Eucalyptus leaves and bark require high and constant heat in order to extract their pigments. A eucalyptus dye bath can take 2–3 hours of boiling to reach a good depth of colour. When used in bundle-dyeing, eucalyptus leaves take much longer (2–3 hours) to produce prints than flowers (30–60 minutes).
- **Storage:** Hang to dry and store indefinitely.
- **Options:** Eucalyptus leaves can be used fresh or dried, but fresh leaves will give the best prints when bundle-dyeing. Soaking the leaves for 12 or more hours can help bring out the pigments in some species.

Black tea (*Camellia sinensis*)

Native to Asia, *Camellia sinensis* is the plant that produces black, green, white and oolong teas. Each tea is prepared differently, and black tea is the most useful for dyeing. Black tea is an excellent dye for beginners, as it contains twice as much tannin as coffee, for example. It is cheap and easy to source worldwide, and makes an extremely colourfast dye. On silk, even without a mordant, black tea can produce a gorgeous golden shade, whereas black tea with iron produces a dark purple.

- **Colours:** Tan, gold, brown, dark purple.
- **Colourfastness:** Excellent.
- **Dyeing:** Leaves – 100% WOF.
- **Heat:** The colour needs to be extracted in boiling water for 15–30 minutes prior to immersing pre-mordanted fibres.
- **Storage:** Store in an airtight container.
- **Options:** A black tea dye bath can be made in the same way you would make a cup of tea. Tea bags can be used in the dye bath to avoid having to strain loose leaves. If you use loose leaves, you can place them inside a tied up piece of muslin (cheesecloth) or similar to avoid having to strain the dye. Tea can also be used for bundle-dyeing in the same way as any other leaf or flower.

Onion (*Allium cepa*)

Onions are ubiquitous culinary plants in many world cuisines, but they also have a long history as dye plants. Onion dye is perfect for beginner dyers who want to use plants from their own kitchen. Brown onion skins produce rich shades of yellow and orange, whereas red onion skins make an olive green. Both colours make olive green when used with iron.

- **Colours:** Yellow, orange, olive green.
- **Colourfastness:** Moderate. A mordant is recommended.
- **Dyeing:** Skins – 100% WOF.
- **Heat:** Onion skins should be boiled for at least 30 minutes.
- **Storage:** Store in an airtight container. Be sure to throw away any wet skins or those that have an odour.
- **Options:** Brown and red onion skins can be used in bundle-dyeing or in a dye bath to make rich shades of yellow and orange. Cutting shapes or hole-punching onion skins can create different patterns when bundle-dyeing.

THE BASICS

Pomegranate (*Punica granatum*)

The pomegranate originated in the Middle East and has long been valued for its medicinal properties and held sacred by many of the world's major religions. It is now a common cooking ingredient worldwide and is loved for its vibrant colour and tart flavour. The colourful juice and bright pink seeds are not suitable for dyeing. It's actually the pomegranate rind that is used for dyeing due to its high tannin content. The dye can be used on its own to create a light yellow, with iron for an olive green/grey or as a mordant for plant fibres. Pomegranate can also be purchased in powder or extract form.

- **Colours:** Yellow, olive green.
- **Colourfastness:** Excellent.
- **Dyeing:** Rinds – 100% WOF; extract – 5% WOF.
- **Heat:** Pomegranate rind requires boiling for at least 60 minutes to extract the yellow dye. The extract can be dissolved into boiling water and fibres immersed immediately.
- **Storage:** Dry or freeze pomegranate rinds. Extract should be stored in an airtight container.
- **Options:** Pomegranate rind is not generally used for bundle-dyeing but the extract can be used sparingly to create a speckled pattern.

Indigo species (*Indigofera*)

Indigo is the most famous of all the natural dyes, and has been used for centuries to create well-loved deep blues. The process for the creation of indigo dyes is completely different to other natural dyes (see pages 138–141). There are three main ingredients in an indigo vat: indigo (fresh leaves or powder), a reducing agent (like sugar) and a base (an alkali like calcium hydroxide). When the indigo is mixed with a reducing agent and a base, the pigment turns from being insoluble (unable to be dissolved into water) to being soluble (dissolvable in water). The fibre can then be dipped into the vat for 10–30 minutes, at which point it will look yellow. As the dye oxidises, it changes to a blue colour. The process can be repeated until the fibre reaches the desired shade. There are many methods of indigo dyeing.

- **Colours:** Blues.
- **Colourfastness:** Excellent. No mordant needed for any fibres.
- **Dyeing:** Indigo is weighed according to the amount of water used, and proportions vary.
- **Heat:** The vat can be started with hot water around 90°C (195°F) and then allowed to cool.
- **Storage:** Indigo powder should be stored in an airtight container.
- **Options:** Indigo can be mixed with other yellow dyes like marigold to make bright greens, which are very difficult to make with other natural dyes.

Other dye sources

- **Leaves:** Comfrey, mountain ash, elder, sorrel, blackberry, weld, pear, bracken, apple, henna, woad, ash, carrot tops, birch, alder, maple, rose, nettle.
- **Flowers:** Geranium, yarrow, hollyhock, dyer's chamomile, cornflower, lily, delphinium, heather, cosmos, oxalis, coreopsis, dahlia, rudbeckia, goldenrod, dandelion.
- **Nuts, seeds and roots:** Annatto seeds, turmeric, alkanet.
- **Insects:** Cochineal, lac.

PART 2

Techniques

Immersion-dyeing

Immersion-dyeing is the most common method of natural dyeing, and it involves immersing fibres in a pot of dye and allowing them to soak until they reach the desired shade. If you want an even, single colour, this is the method for you. Although this seems like a simple way to dye, there are a number of things that can trip you up and cause the dye to be blotchy. If you aren't especially concerned about a 'perfect' dye job, don't worry about the points below; part of the beauty of dyeing is that it is done by hand and results in a hand-dyed look, so try to embrace any imperfections. However, these tips will help you achieve a good result:

- **Scouring**: The fibre must be completely clean. If you have a fabric that has marks or stains, the dye is likely to be darker in those areas. Scouring is particularly important for immersion-dyeing. This is the reason that I don't recommend immersion-dyeing second-hand or vintage textiles, as they are likely to have stains, even if they are not apparent before dyeing. Other dyeing techniques work better for second-hand clothing.

- **Mordanting**: The fibre must be evenly mordanted to avoid ending up with patchy spots. This means that when mordanting, you need to ensure that the fibre has plenty of room to move in the pot and that it is stirred frequently. Make sure that there are no air bubbles under the fibre that prevent it from absorbing the mordant properly.

- **Stirring**: You must stir the pot when dyeing to ensure that parts of the fibre aren't sitting above water level and consequently absorbing less dye. You will also need to use plenty of water so that the fibre isn't bunched up, as this will result in blotches.

- **Contamination**: You need to be careful not to contaminate the dyed fibre with any pH modifiers or iron. It's important to ensure your workspace is cleaned of any acids, alkalis or metals that could touch the fibre and result in spots and marks.

TECHNIQUES

HAND DYED DESIGNS

TECHNIQUES

Immersion-dyeing with raw plant materials

Method:

1. Make sure the fibre has been scoured or hot washed according to the instructions on page 18.

2. If you have dried the fibre, pre-wet it for roughly 60 minutes by soaking it in a bucket of cold water.

3. Pre-mordant the fibre according to the instructions on pages 24–25, unless you have chosen not to use a mordant.

4. Fill a stainless steel pot with water and bring it to a simmer. The amount of water you use will depend on how much space the fibre needs to move. It's important that the fibre can move freely in the pot. Using more water may cause the dye to be more diluted but it won't affect the end result.

5. Add the dye plant to the pot at 100% WOF (e.g., 100 g [3.5 oz] onion skins for 100 g [3.5 oz] fibre).

6. Allow the dye to heat until you can see the pigment extracted into the water. For some plants this can take just 10 minutes, whereas others you may need to heat for up to 2 hours. Certain plants require care when it comes to heat and will become muddy or lose their pigment if the water is too hot. Generally, more delicate plant components (flower petals) can't withstand high heats, whereas those that are more robust (bark, nuts and wood) require high heats. Refer to pages 40–66 to check the temperature your chosen plant material requires.

7. Turn the heat off and use a strainer to remove any pieces of the plant so you are left with a clear dye.

8. Add the pre-wetted fibre to the pot, ensuring there is enough water for it to move around freely. You can choose to return the pot to the heat, or place the lid on top and allow the fibre to soak in the pot off the heat. Remember, heat speeds up the dyeing process but isn't essential.

9. Check the fibre after 60 minutes to see how the shade is developing. You can leave it in the dye for up to 24 hours to get the deepest shade.

10. When you're happy with the shade, remove the fibre from the pot and rinse it in cold water using a gentle detergent.

11. Hang it to dry and iron if necessary.

Immersion-dyeing with extracts or powders

The processes for using extracts and powders are very similar. The only difference is that extracts almost completely dissolve in water and usually do not need to be strained. Powders generally need to be heated for longer and do not dissolve.

Method:

1. Make sure the fibre has been scoured or hot washed according to the instructions on page 18.

2. If you have dried the fibre, pre-wet it for roughly 60 minutes by soaking it in a bucket of cold water.

3. Pre-mordant the fibre according to the instructions on pages 24–25, unless you have chosen not to use a mordant.

4. Fill a stainless steel pot with water and bring it to just below boiling. The amount of water you use will depend on the weight of the fibre and how much space the fibre needs to move freely. Using more water may cause the dye to be more diluted but it won't affect the end result.

5. Measure the dye extract or powder according to the manufacturer's instructions. For example, if you are dyeing a 200 g (7 oz) t-shirt with madder, you might use 20% WOF (40 g [1.4 oz] madder). To achieve a deeper or paler shade, use more or less of the extract or powder accordingly.

6. Be aware of any specific heat or pH requirements. Although most powders and extracts provide beautiful shades regardless of heat or pH, there are some which need more care. For example, madder thrives in hard water/alkaline conditions, so you may want to add a pinch of sodium carbonate to make the water more alkaline. Madder also produces the best colours when it's kept below boiling point.

7. **Extracts:** Dissolve the extract in the hot water, then add the fibre to the water. Extracts are very potent powders that dissolve into the water and create a dye bath immediately, so you can add the fibre as soon as the extract is dissolved. You don't need to strain the dye bath before immersing the fibre.

TECHNIQUES

8. **Powders:** Put the powder in the hot water and leave it for about 15 minutes, then check the colour by putting a piece of scrap fabric in the dye bath. It may take slightly longer to see the dye bath develop with a dye powder than with an extract, but it is still generally faster than using raw plants. Strain the dye bath to get rid of any plant material, as it may cause unwanted spots on your fabric. Then immerse the fibre in the dye bath.
9. You can choose to return the pot to the heat, or place the lid on top and allow the fibre to soak in the pot off the heat. Remember, heat speeds up the dyeing process but isn't essential.
10. Check the fibre after 60 minutes to see how the shade is developing. You can leave it in the dye for up to 24 hours to get the deepest shade.
11. When you're happy with the shade, remove the fibre from the pot and rinse it in cold water using a gentle detergent.
12. Hang it to dry and iron if necessary.

Cold water immersion-dyeing

This method can be used when dyeing with raw plants, extracts or powders. However, it works most efficiently with extracts or powders, as raw plants can take a very long time to release their colour without heat. The main difference is in the preparation of the dye bath and the duration of time the fabric soaks in the dye.

Method:

1. Make sure the fibre has been scoured or hot washed according to the instructions on page 18.

2. If you have dried the fibre, make sure you pre-wet it for roughly 60 minutes by soaking it in a bucket of cold water.

3. Pre-mordant the fibre according to the instructions on pages 24–25, unless you have chosen not to use a mordant.

4. Prepare the dye bath by following whichever of the methods on pages 76–77 is appropriate to the type of dye you are using (raw plant, extract or powder), and allow the dye to cool. Dye baths for raw plants and powders require a little hot water initially to extract the pigment, but extracts can be dissolved by being mixed into cold water.

5. Immerse the wet, pre-mordanted fibre in the dye bath and allow it to soak for at least 24–36 hours, or until it reaches your desired shade. Weigh down the fabric with a ceramic plate or another heavy, non-reactive object to prevent it from floating above the surface and producing a patchy result.

6. Stir as often as you can, replacing the weights afterwards.

7. When you're happy with the shade, remove the fibre from the pot and rinse it in cold water using a gentle detergent.

8. Hang it to dry and iron if necessary.

Bundle-dyeing

Bundle-dyeing, also known as eco-printing, is a process that involves permanently printing the shapes and colours from plants directly onto fabric. This technique is a beautiful way to extract the colours from plants, and also to use their shapes to create unique patterns. Once you get the hang of it, this is one of the easiest ways to dye fabric, as it is very forgiving, covers stains and marks and can be redone over and over again until you're satisfied with the pattern.

Bundle-dyeing is perfect for plant components like flowers, leaves, and onion skins, as well as natural dye extracts and powders. Dried and pressed flowers will produce the clearest prints. Bundle-dyeing doesn't work so well with larger plant materials like avocado stones, bark or wood since it's difficult to roll these bulky plants inside the fabric.

TECHNIQUES

Bundle-dyeing fabric

You can use any natural fibre for this process, but silk will give you the brightest, clearest prints. If you would like the base colour of your fabric to be a different colour, you can dye it first in a dye bath according to the instructions on pages 70–79.

Method:

1. Make sure the fabric has been scoured or hot washed according to the instructions on page 18.

2. If you have dried the fibre, pre-wet it for roughly 60 minutes by soaking it in a bucket of cold water.

3. Pre-mordant the fabric according to the instructions on pages 24–25, unless you have chosen not to use a mordant.

4. Lay the wet fabric on a table or the floor, making sure to flatten it as much as possible.

5. Collect some flowers, leaves and/or other plant materials. These can be fresh or dried. I suggest trying a variety and experimenting to see which you like best.

6. Arrange the plant materials over the entire fabric (see page 83). If you are using a large piece of fabric, you can lay the plant materials on half of the fabric and fold the other half of the fabric over it.

7. If you wish, add some natural dye extracts or powders; use them sparingly until you understand the effect they will have. Some can be very potent, so a little goes a long way.

8. Roll the fabric into a tight bundle. You can use a wooden dowel or plastic stick to help in the rolling process. Ensure you are pressing firmly when rolling so the plants are pressed as closely as possible to the fabric. Try to remove creases where you can, as sometimes they can be hard to get out after steaming.

9. Tie the bundle tightly with string or rubber bands.

10. Place the bundle in a steamer pot for at least 30 minutes and then pull back a corner to assess how the plants are transferring. If more transfer is needed, steam for another 30 minutes. Alternatively you can put the bundle in a pot of water or dye instead of the steamer pot. This can create some interesting effects and add some extra colour, but the prints may not be as crisp and clear as they are when using a steamer pot.

11. Remove the bundle from the pot and allow it to cool before unwrapping it and brushing off the plant material.
12. Rinse the fabric in cold water using a gentle detergent and hang to dry.

> **Tip:** You can add some rusty metal into the bundle to get the effect of an iron mordant on parts of the fabric. Try using rusty nails or other pieces of metal you might have around and lay them over the fabric with the plant materials. When you unwrap the bundle you will notice dark patterns where the iron has reacted with the dye plants.

TECHNIQUES

Bundle-dyeing pre-made garments

Bundle-dyeing pre-made garments is different to bundle-dyeing a flat piece of fabric. While most of the steps are the same, there are a few things you'll need to take into account to ensure all parts of the fabric are dyed. You can use any natural fibre for this process, but silk will give you the brightest, clearest prints. If you would like the base colour of your fabric to be a different colour, you can dye it first in a dye bath according to the instructions on pages 70–79.

Method:

1. Make sure the fabric has been scoured or hot washed according to the instructions on page 18.
2. If you have dried the fibre, pre-wet it for roughly 60 minutes by soaking it in a bucket of cold water.
3. Pre-mordant the garment according to the instructions on pages 24–25, unless you have chosen not to use a mordant.
4. Lay the wet garment on a table or the floor, making sure to flatten it as much as possible.
5. Collect some flowers, leaves and/or other plant materials. These can be fresh or dried. I suggest trying a variety and experimenting to see which you like best.
6. Arrange the plant materials over one side of the garment or in the middle of the garment.
7. If you wish, add some natural dye extracts or powders; use them sparingly until you understand the effect they will have. Some can be very potent, so a little goes a long way.
8. When you have placed the plant materials on one side or in the middle of the garment, fold the opposite sides on top (see page 93).
9. Place another layer of plant materials on top. Continue folding and placing more layers of dye materials until you are ready to roll the garment.
10. Roll the fabric into a tight bundle. You can use a wooden dowel or plastic stick to help in the rolling process. Ensure you are pressing firmly when rolling so the plants are pressed as closely as possible to the fabric. Try to remove creases where you can, as sometimes they can be hard to get out after steaming.
11. Tie the bundle tightly with string or rubber bands.

12. Place the bundle in a steamer pot for at least 30 minutes and then pull back a corner to assess how the plants are transferring. If more transfer is needed, steam for another 30 minutes.
13. Remove the bundle from the pot and allow it to cool before unwrapping it and brushing off the plant material.
14. Rinse the fabric in cold water using a gentle detergent and hang to dry.

Printing with leaves

Although we largely use the same processes for bundle-dyeing with leaves as we do with any other materials, there are a few extra tricks that can make leaf printing easier. Many people want a very clear leaf print, as opposed to a more abstract, speckled bundle-dyed print. Here are some tips that can help you achieve that:

– **Soak the leaves in water, dye or mordant:** This will improve results for some leaves, although it doesn't work for all of them. Soaking in water can help produce clearer prints, but like everything in natural dyeing, experimentation is key. When a leaf is soaked in dye, it may leave a brighter (or different colour) print than its original pigment would allow. When a leaf is soaked in iron, it may work as a colour modifier and give a darker colour print. You can also get this result by mordanting the fabric with iron.

– **Damp but not wet:** Although we usually use wet fabric, it is possible to use dry fabric when using soaked leaves. If you do choose to use wet fabric, make sure you have wrung out as much water as possible. Too much water in the fabric leads to muddy prints. This is another reason I always steam my bundles instead of boiling them.

– **Reduce creases:** The bundle needs to be tight and flat. Ensure the fabric isn't creased prior to laying your leaves, and roll it around a wooden dowel or plastic stick so that the leaves are pressed very tightly to the fabric. As much as possible, make sure you are not creating creases as you roll, as this can result in patchy leaf prints or prints that appear 'broken'. It is easier to print with leaves on a flat piece of fabric than a pre-made garment.

– **Bundle tightly:** Make sure you use a liberal amount of string to tie the entire bundle tightly. If you miss a section of the bundle, it's likely that the print underneath won't be as deep in colour.

– **Lay front side down:** For the best colour results, lay your leaves front facing down. The reverse side of the leaf may also produce decent colour, but I find that front down is best.

TECHNIQUES

Using an iron blanket

In order to get a darker background behind leaf or flower prints, lay an iron blanket over the top of the fabric before rolling and tying. The blanket can be any piece of fabric, but a cheap cotton calico or canvas works well as it can hold more mordant. When the fabric is already mordanted with tannin, the iron will react with the tannin to create a dark blue/grey.

Method:

1. Pre-mordant your target fabric with tannin alone (or another mordant plus dye depending on the colour you want) according to the instructions on pages 24–25.

2. Rinse the fabric and wring dry.

3. Mordant the 'blanket' in iron according to the instructions on page 28.

4. Lay the target fabric flat on a table or floor and place the plant materials on top according to the instructions on pages 80–95.

5. Lay the iron-mordanted blanket over the plant materials so they are sandwiched between the target fabric and the blanket.

6. Roll the fabric into a tight bundle. You can use a wooden dowel or plastic stick to help in the rolling process. Ensure you are pressing firmly when rolling so the plants are pressed as closely as possible to the fabric. Try to remove creases where you can, as sometimes they can be hard to get out after steaming.

7. Tie the bundle tightly with string or rubber bands.

8. Place the bundle in a steamer pot for at least 30 minutes or longer if necessary. The amount of time in the steamer pot depends on the requirements of the plants you are using.

9. Remove the bundle from the pot and allow it to cool.

10. Untie the string and remove the iron blanket.

11. Peel off the plant materials and rinse the fabric in cold water using a gentle detergent.

12. Hang it to dry and iron to remove creases if necessary.

Using a dye blanket

A dye blanket works in the same way as an iron blanket except rather than carrying iron, which will react with the dyes in the target fabric, it carries a dye of your choice. The blanket can be any piece of fabric but a cheap cotton calico or canvas works well as it can hold more dye. This is a beautiful way to bundle-dye with a background other than white.

Method:

1. Pre-mordant your target fabric with a mordant of your choice according to the instructions on pages 24–25.
2. Rinse the fabric and wring dry.
3. Dye the 'blanket' in a dye of your choice according to the instructions on pages 70–79.
4. Lay the target fabric flat on a table or the floor and place the plant materials on top according to the instructions on pages 80–95.
5. Lay the dye blanket over the plant materials so they are sandwiched between the target fabric and the blanket.
6. Roll the fabric into a tight bundle. You can use a wooden dowel or plastic stick to help in the rolling process. Ensure you are pressing firmly when rolling so the plants are pressed as closely as possible to the fabric. Try to remove creases where you can, as sometimes they can be hard to get out after steaming.
7. Tie the bundle tightly with string or rubber bands.
8. Place the bundle in a steamer pot for at least 30 minutes or longer if necessary. The amount of time in the steamer pot depends on the requirements of the plants you are using.
9. Remove the bundle from the pot and allow it to cool.
10. Untie the string and remove the dye blanket.
11. Peel off the plant materials and rinse the fabric in cold water using a gentle detergent.
12. Hang it to dry and iron to remove creases if necessary.

TECHNIQUES

Using a barrier

During the steaming stage, colours from the plants can often seep through layers of the fabric, leaving an 'imperfect' print. This is less of a problem with heavier fabric like cotton canvas where you will likely only get the print on one side, but is common when using most types of silk or other lightweight fabrics. To prevent this from happening, you can use a piece of material that we call a 'barrier'. This can be either a thick piece of fabric, some baking paper, or even a layer of recycled plastic that can be placed underneath, between or on top of layers of fabric.

Method:

1. Lay the barrier flat on the table. Ensure it's the same or similar size as your fabric.
2. Lay the washed and mordanted fabric on top of the barrier and proceed through the bundle-dyeing steps on pages 98–99.
3. Lay another barrier on top of the fabric after you have applied the plants and/or powders (optional).
4. Roll the bundle according to the bundle-dyeing instructions on pages 80–95.
5. Dye, then steam the bundle.
6. When the bundle is ready, remove it from the pot and allow it to cool, then remove the barriers and plant materials.
7. Rinse the fabric in cold water using a gentle detergent and hang to dry.

Dyeing with rust

As we know from pages 29–30, we can make an iron mordant using rusty objects. But we can also use the rich brown/orange pigments in rust to permanently dye fabric. This is not only a very colourfast method, it is also incredibly simple. There is no need for heat or water, only rust, fabric and vinegar. This is a fun way to try dyeing without having to worry about making a pot of dye or steaming the fabric. You can also place rusty objects on top of the fabric when bundle-dyeing or directly in your dye bath to create a darker dye.

Method:

1. Make sure the fibre has been scoured or hot washed according to the instructions on page 18. You can use it wet or leave it to dry before proceeding. It is not necessary to mordant for this technique.

2. Spray the fabric with vinegar.

3. Lay the rusty objects over the fabric, folding or rolling if necessary to make sure as much of the fabric as possible is coming into contact with the rusty objects.

4. Place the fabric either in a bag, an old bucket or on a plate (not used for food) and allow it to sit in a cool place out of the sun for at least 24 hours, but preferably 48 hours. Check on the fabric occasionally to see how the colour is developing. Do not leave it for longer than 48 hours, as the fabric may begin to deteriorate.

5. When the colour has reached the desired depth of shade, remove the rusty objects and wash the fabric in cold water using a gentle detergent.

6. At this point you can add some inks, bundle-dye or immerse the fabric in a dye bath if you would like to combine techniques.

7. Hang the fabric to dry and iron to remove creases if necessary.

TECHNIQUES

Resist-dyeing

Resist-dyeing is a technique that allows us to create specific patterns by using materials such as thread, string, plastic, paste, wax, or wood to prevent the dye from reaching all parts of the fabric. The hippie tie-dye we all recognise from the 1960s and 70s is a type of resist-dyeing. The various methods in this book are all inspired by traditional Japanese shibori, but different forms of resist-dyeing have been used throughout the world, from Peru to Nigeria to India, dating back thousands of years. The oldest form of tie-dye dates back to 4000 BCE in Northern India. Although traditionally resist techniques were most often used with indigo, any natural dye can be used. By using resist-dyeing techniques we can create repeated patterns like swirls, circles, stripes and squares in two or more colours.

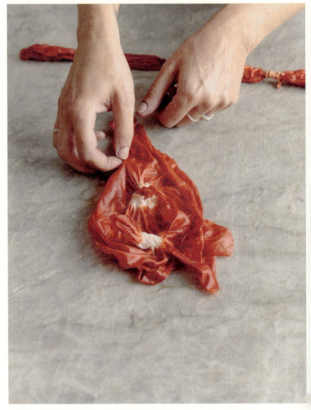

Tie-dyeing using string or rubber bands

There are many different ways to tie-dye, with most methods inspired by Japanese shibori. You can use any natural fibre for this process. I recommend using heat in your dye bath, even if you turn it off when you immerse the fabric. If you don't want to use heat, you can make a dye using cold water (see page 79). As always, fabrics need to be pre-washed, and can be used straightaway or dried for later use. As with other processes, fabrics need to be pre-wetted for this technique.

Method:

1. Pre-mordant the fabric according to the instructions on pages 24–25.
2. Choose a basic pattern you'd like to achieve, such as scrunching, lines, swirls or circles.
3. Tie parts of the fabric following the images opposite. For a high contrast effect, be sure to tie the rubber bands or string very tightly. This will prevent the dye from reaching the tied parts of the fabric. String or rubber bands which are tied too loosely can result in only a faint contrast.
4. Create a dye bath using materials of your choice.
5. Once you have tied all parts of the fabric or garment that you want to resist the dye, immerse the fabric in the dye bath.
6. Leave the fabric in the dye bath for at least 1 hour, or up to 24 hours.
7. Remove the fabric from the dye bath with the string or rubber bands still in place and rinse it in cold water.
8. If you plan to use a modifier such as iron, an alkali or an acid, do this prior to untying the string or rubber bands.
9. Untie the string or rubber bands and rinse the fabric again, then hang it to dry and iron if necessary.

> **Tip:** Sometimes string and rubber bands can leave creases, especially on silk. These will most likely disappear with time and use, but if you would like to try to get them out immediately, use an iron on the setting appropriate for your fabric. It sometimes helps to use a spray bottle filled with water and spray the fabric as you iron. You can also use a dryer to remove the creases.

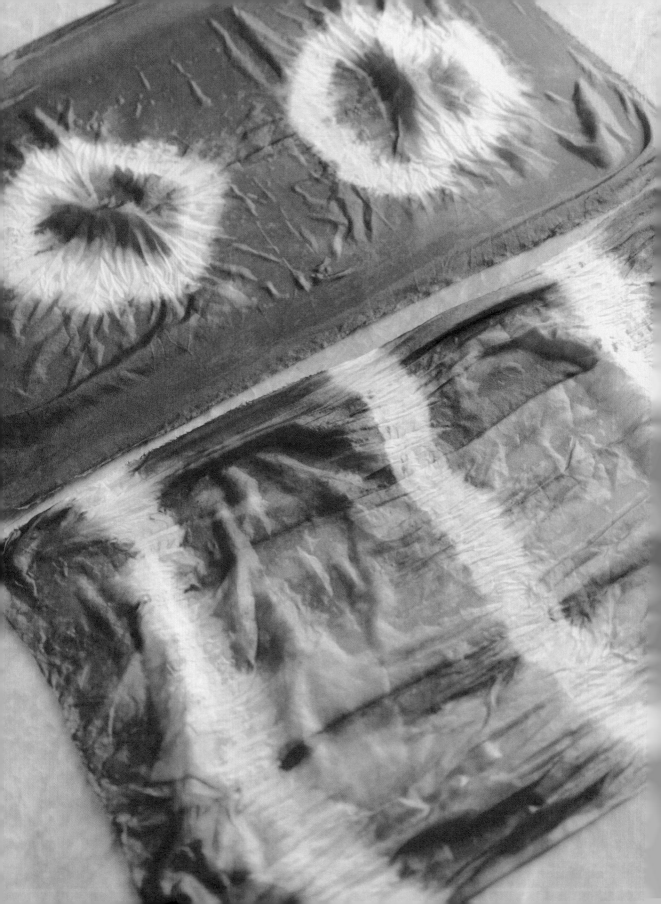

TECHNIQUES

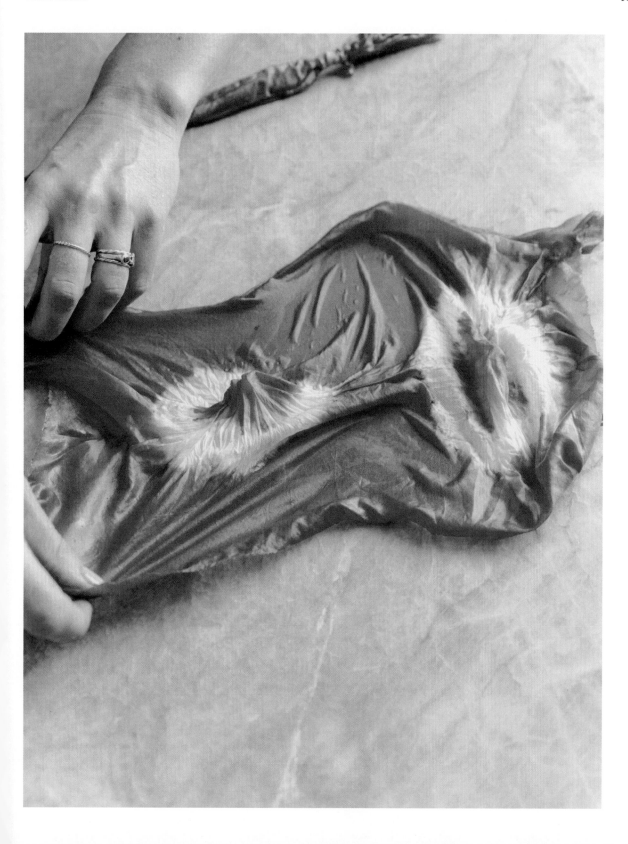

Shape resist-dyeing

This technique is called *itajime* in Japanese, which translates as 'board clamping'. Rather than using string or thread to prevent the dye from reaching the fabric, we use a pair of solid shapes (wood, metal or plastic) clamped tightly on either side of the fabric. Again, this is traditionally done with indigo, but any natural dye bath can be used. You can use purchased *itajime* shibori shapes, or any pair of shapes that you find in your home, such as jar lids, wooden squares or any other pairs of firm wooden or plastic shapes. If you choose to use metal like a tin can or jar lid, be aware that you may see some colour changes when the metal reacts with the natural dye. You can use any natural fibre for this technique. As usual, fabrics need to be pre-washed, and can be used straightaway or dried for later use.

Method:

1. Pre-mordant the fabric according to the instructions on pages 24–25.
2. If you have dried the fibre, pre-wet it for roughly 60 minutes by soaking it in a bucket of cold water.
3. Fold the fabric or garment neatly until you have a square that is slightly bigger than your shapes.
4. Place one shape on either side of the folded fabric and hold it in place using a clamp (I find that a spring clamp works well).
5. Prepare the dye bath. I recommend using heat in the dye bath whenever possible, even if you turn it off when you immerse your fabric. If you don't want to use heat, make a dye using cold water (see page 79).
6. Immerse the fabric with the shape attached in the dye bath.
7. Leave the fabric in the dye bath for at least 1 hour, or up to 24 hours.
8. Remove the fabric from the pot and rinse it in cold water prior to removing the shapes. If you plan to use a modifier like iron, an alkali or an acid, do this prior to removing the shapes.
9. Remove the clamp and the shapes.
10. Rinse the fabric again, then hang it to dry and iron if necessary.

HAND DYED DESIGNS

TECHNIQUES

Painting with dyes and mordants

Painting with mordants involves using a paintbrush to apply the mordant to select parts of the fabric either before or after dyeing. Painting with dyes is a very similar process and involves making an ink that is essentially a very concentrated dye. This is applied directly onto select parts of the fabric, instead of placing the entire fabric in a dye bath. This is a beautiful way to apply many different colours to one piece of fabric in a controlled design. Similar techniques have been used throughout history, particularly in Indian block printing, to create intricate designs. It is a way to have more control and creativity over the designs and patterns you create using natural colours.

There are various ways to create a mordant or dye 'paint', including simply mixing the mordant or dye with a small amount of water and applying it to dry fabric with a paintbrush. However, when only using water, the solution can be too thin, causing the patterns to bleed, which is why I suggest using a binder as per the recipes that follow. Keep in mind that you can omit the binder, or add more binder depending on the consistency you want. The solution can then be applied to the fabric using a paintbrush, a woodblock, by screen-printing, dripping, spraying or using various other tools and methods. It's worth noting that, unlike dye paints, mordant paints don't store well and need to be discarded after use.

BINDERS

When making an ink with natural dyes, we sometimes use a binder or gum to thicken the solution. These include gum tragacanth, gum arabic and guar gum. When a gum is mixed with water it can take some time and vigorous stirring or blending to remove the lumps. For this reason I prefer to make gum paste in a batch prior to mixing it with natural dyes.

GUM ARABIC

Also known as acacia gum, gum arabic is made from the sap of some types of acacia tree, most commonly *Acacia senegal*. It is a common ingredient used in the food industry and as a binder for making paint. It is readily dissolved in water without the use of a blender and easier to remove from the fabric afterwards without using wheat bran; however, it is more costly.

GUAR GUM

Guar gum is a thickening agent made from guar beans. It is also commonly used as a treatment for digestive issues, high cholesterol, and high blood pressure. It is cheaper than gum arabic and less is needed to make a paste, but it can be difficult to remove lumps. I recommend using an electric blender to make the solution smooth. You can use the blender you use for food preparation as long as you're not mixing in any inedible mordants or dyes.

The method for making gum arabic and guar gum solutions is essentially the same, although the ingredients and quantities differ.

TECHNIQUES

Pre-mixed binders

GUM ARABIC

Ingredients:

20–50 g (0.7–1.8 oz) gum arabic

100 ml (3.4 fl oz) hot water

Method:

1. Place the gum in a jar or bowl.
2. Add the water.
3. Stir them together thoroughly to make a paste. This can take some time.
4. If you can't remove the lumps, let the solution sit for 20–30 minutes. Stir again or put the solution in a blender until it is smooth.
5. Proceed to make your paint. The paint can be stored for up to 3 months in the jar.

GUAR GUM

Ingredients:

2 g (0.07 oz) guar gum

100 ml (3.4 fl oz) boiling water

See method above.

TECHNIQUES

Painting with mordants

PAINTING WITH IRON AND ALUMINIUM

Iron paint ingredients:

30 ml (1 fl oz) hot water

2 g (0.07 oz) iron (ferrous sulphate)

80 ml (2.6 fl oz) pre-mixed guar gum solution (see recipe on page 117)

Aluminium paint ingredients:

80 ml (2.6 fl oz) pre-mixed guar gum solution (see recipe on page 117)

10 g (0.35 oz) aluminium (any)

30 ml (1 fl oz) hot water

Method:

1. Add hot water to a jar or bowl.
2. Add the mordant (iron or aluminium) and stir until dissolved. To make a modifier paint, substitute the mordant for a modifier instead.
3. Add the guar gum solution and stir. In the absence of guar gum, substitute with more hot water for a thinner solution.
4. The 'paint' can now be used either on dry undyed fabric or dry pre-dyed fabric. Aluminium should be used prior to dyeing. Iron can be used before or after dyeing.
5. After painting your desired design, allow the paint to dry fully (usually at least 24 hours). It will feel slightly stiff. Do not proceed to the next step until it is completely dry.
6. Rinse the fabric to remove any paint that has not bonded with the fabric. This is best done in running water rather than in a bucket or sink. If you skip this step, the paint can move to other parts of the fabric and cause a muddy or blurry pattern. You can also use a washing machine for this process. Skip the next steps if you have used pre-dyed fabric.
7. Prepare the dye bath according to the instructions on pages 70–79. I advise using hot water if possible.
8. Immerse the wet, painted fabric into the dye bath and allow it to soak for at least 60 minutes. You will see the pattern emerge almost immediately. Remember to stir it regularly for an even dye job.
9. Remove the fabric from the dye bath, rinse in cold water and hang it to dry.

> **Tip:** If you want the background to remain white while still being able to see the painted pattern, use a dye that is almost invisible unless used with a mordant (clear tannins such as tara or gallnut, or other dyes like sappanwood that are unsuccessful without a mordant). If you would like the background to be dyed too, use a stronger dye that works well without a mordant (like cutch, fustic, avocado, black tea, or onion skins). As usual, fabrics need to be pre-washed, and then must be dried.

PAINTING WITH SOY

For this method, you will need to use pre-washed (scoured) fabric which is not mordanted. The fabric must be undyed and completely dry before painting. A combination of soy and guar gum will achieve defined lines. If you would prefer less defined lines, you can omit the gum and paint directly with soy. Soy (or iron) paint solutions can also be used for block printing, screen printing, spraying or dripping.

Ingredients:

50 ml (1.7 fl oz) pre-mixed guar gum solution (see recipe page 117)

50 ml (1.7 fl oz) soy milk (store-bought or home-made, without additives such as oil)

Method:

1. Mix the guar gum ahead of time in a jar, bowl or cup.
2. In another jar, combine the soy milk with the guar gum and stir. Add more gum if needed to achieve a thicker paint.
3. Paint your design onto the dry fabric with a paintbrush. The paint will be almost invisible.
4. Allow the paint to dry completely (usually at least 24 hours).
5. Rinse the fabric in cold running water to remove any excess soy or gum.
6. Prepare the dye bath according to the instructions on pages 70–79.
7. Immerse the fabric in the dye bath. I recommend using a dye high in tannin for the most colourfast results.
8. Allow the fabric to soak for at least 30 minutes, stirring regularly. You will see the pattern come up almost immediately. The longer you leave the fabric in the pot the deeper the colours will become, but keep in mind that unless you stir constantly, you may end up with a blotchy result.
9. Remove the fabric from the dye bath and rinse in cold water. Allow it to dry and iron if necessary.

PAINTING PRE-MADE GARMENTS

When painting an existing garment as opposed to a flat piece of fabric, you will need to take precautions so that the paint doesn't seep through to other layers. For example, when painting a pair of pants, it might be necessary to put a protective layer inside the legs before painting the front side. After the front side has dried, you can then turn the pants over and paint the back. This prevents unwanted marks. You can use a piece of cardboard, a thick piece of fabric, baking paper or a flat piece of plastic as a protective layer.

TECHNIQUES

Painting with dyes

NATURAL DYE EXTRACT INK

Ingredients:

1 teaspoon natural dye extract

10 ml (0.3 fl oz) boiling water

40 ml (1.3 fl oz) pre-mixed guar gum

gentle detergent

Method:

1. Mordant the pre-washed fabric according to the instructions on pages 24–25 and allow it to dry.

2. Mix the natural dye extract with the hot water. Stir until the extract is dissolved completely.

3. Add the pre-mixed guar gum. This will keep your lines crisp and clear. Do not add too much gum, as it can prevent the pigments from adhering to the fibres.

4. Spread the fabric flat on a table or the floor. Make sure it is dry or only slightly damp to prevent the colours from spreading to unwanted areas on the fabric.

5. Apply the ink to the fabric either with a paintbrush, or by screen printing, block printing, spraying or dripping.

6. Allow the paint to dry completely (usually 24 hours).

7. Heat set the colours by using one of the options listed on page 127 (dryer, iron or steaming).

8. If you have the time, this technique benefits from leaving the fabric 1–2 weeks (or more) to cure.

9. Wash the fabric thoroughly using a gentle detergent. Allow it to dry and iron if necessary.

Tip: If you have dye paint left over, you can save it for later use. As long as it is kept in an airtight container in a cool place, it will last for months. Over time you may notice mould appearing on the surface, in which case you can either scrape it off and use what remains, or discard the dye and make another batch.

HEAT SETTING

When painting directly onto fabric with a natural dye ink, it's necessary to use heat to 'set' the colours for maximum colourfastness. There are four ways to do this:

- **Professional bullet steamer**: Most people don't own a bullet steamer, but if you do, this is the best option. Place the fabric in the steamer for 60 minutes.

- **Hand iron**: This can feel laborious, but you can iron in increments of 10 minutes for a total of 60 minutes. This method is best for smaller pieces of fabric.

- **Hot dryer**: Probably the simplest and easiest option, a dryer won't give the same level of heat as the other methods but does help to improve colourfastness, especially if the fabric has been cured post-painting.

- **Steam in a pot**: This is the easiest and most effective option for anyone who doesn't own a bullet steamer. Wrap the fabric in calico or baking paper to prevent colour spreading to other parts of the fabric and place it in a steamer pot the way you would when bundle-dyeing (see image on page 85). Allow it to steam for 60 minutes.

TECHNIQUES

RAW PLANT DYE INK

Similar to the process of immersion-dyeing with raw plants outlined on page 73, in order to make an ink using a raw plant you will first need to extract the pigment into water. Although all plants are different, a good rule of thumb is to use 50 g (1.8 oz) plant material in 500 ml (17 fl oz) water. As always, fabrics need to be pre-washed, and can be used straightaway or dried for later use.

Ingredients:

50 g (1.8 oz) plant material

500 ml (17 fl oz) water

1 g (0.03 oz) guar gum

Method:

1. Mordant the fabric according to the instructions on pages 24–25 and allow it to dry.

2. Combine the plant material with the water in a pot.

3. Simmer the solution and reduce until you have roughly 100 ml (3.4 fl oz) liquid (after straining).

4. If you would like to thicken the ink to prevent it bleeding, add the guar gum. This will keep your lines crisp and clear. Stir it thoroughly and leave it to sit for 30 minutes.

5. Spread the fabric flat on a table or the floor. Make sure it is dry or only slightly damp to prevent the colours from spreading to unwanted areas on the fabric. If you would like an abstract watercolour effect, you can use fabric that has been wrung dry.

6. Paint your design onto the fabric with a paintbrush.

7. Allow the paint to dry completely (usually 24 hours). Leave it to cure for as long as possible if you have the time (2–3 weeks).

8. Heat set the colours by using one of the options listed on page 127 (dryer, iron or steaming).

9. Wash the fabric thoroughly using a gentle detergent. Allow it to dry and iron if necessary.

TECHNIQUES

PAINTING ON OTHER SURFACES

The paint techniques outlined in this section can also be used on other surfaces, such as paper, wood, leather or a stretched canvas. All of these materials can be mordanted using the instructions on pages 24–25. Although natural paints can't be heated in a kiln, they can be used on pieces of air-dried or kiln-dried clay as long as the pieces are not used to hold liquids.

How to make a lake pigment

A lake pigment is a powdered pigment made by precipitating a natural dye with a mordant, most commonly aluminium. Precipitation occurs when the water-soluble pigment transforms into an insoluble solid. In this case, the pigment and the aluminium bond together and fall to the bottom of the solution. When the precipitate falls to the bottom of the pot or jar, it can be filtered, spread onto a flat surface, dried and ground up into powder form. Lake pigments are made in order to extract the colour from plants and use them to mix with a binder to create a paint (as opposed to a water-soluble natural ink). Making a lake pigment is also a way to reuse any leftover dye baths rather than pouring the contents down the sink.

You will need:

4 parts dry dye material

2 parts aluminium

1 part sodium carbonate

1 stainless steel pot

1 glass jar at least 1 litre (34 fl oz) capacity

3 smaller jars

300 ml (10 fl oz) hot water

1 pipette or baster

1 funnel or a piece of fabric and a rubber band

1 coffee filter

mortar and pestle

Method:

1. Make a dye in the same way as you would for dyeing fabric. Using hot water in the stainless steel pot, extract the pigment from your chosen plant or powder according to the instructions on pages 70–79, or dissolve an extract into the water. When you are satisfied with the colour of the dye solution, let it cool for a few minutes so it's not boiling and pour it into the large jar.

2. Mix the aluminium with 150 ml (5 fl oz) of the hot water in one of the smaller jars. Stir until it dissolves.

3. Mix the sodium carbonate with 150 ml (5 fl oz) of the hot water in one of the smaller jars. Stir until it dissolves.

4. Add the aluminium solution to the dye in the large jar.

5. Gradually add the sodium carbonate solution to the dye in the large jar and stir. This part of the process will create a large amount of foam that is likely to overflow from the jar, so make sure to do this in a sink or outside.

6. Stir the solution to reduce the foam.

7. When you have added all of the sodium carbonate solution, leave the jar to sit until the precipitate falls to the bottom. This will occur within 2–24 hours. If there is still a lot of pigment in the water you can add more aluminium and sodium carbonate accordingly.

8. Filter the precipitate by emptying out the water sitting on top and adding more clean water. Repeat this process until there is no pigment left in the water on top.

TECHNIQUES

9. Use the pipette or baster to remove the water on top of the jar, or carefully pour it off without pouring out the precipitate at the bottom.

10. Use the funnel or the piece of fabric with rubber band tied around on the top of one of the smaller jars (see page 134) to hold the weight of the solution in the coffee filter.

11. Pour the dye solution into the coffee filter and leave it to drain the remaining water into the jar (at least 2 hours). It's important to dry the lake pigment as much as possible. If there is too much water left in the solution it will take longer to dry.

12. Remove the coffee filter and lay it completely flat. Spread the lake pigment out over the filter paper roughly 1 mm (0.03 in) thick. If it's too thick, it will take longer to dry.

13. Leave the pigment to dry. It will start to crack and look like dried earth.

14. When the pigment is completely dry, scrape it off the filter into the mortar and pestle.

15. Grind the pigment into a fine powder and prepare a binder to make a paint. The paint can now be used on fabric, paper and wood.

16. Store the paint in a cool dry place.

TECHNIQUES

TECHNIQUES

Preparing an indigo vat

You will need:

gentle detergent

natural fibre of your choice

10 litres (350 fl oz) water, just below boiling

1 stainless steel pot

50 g (1.8 oz) indigo powder

100 g (3.5 oz) calcium hydroxide

150 g (5.5 oz) fructose

150 ml (5.5 fl oz) boiling water

3 jars or containers

tongs

Method:

1. Pre-wash the fibre in a hot cycle in the washing machine using a gentle detergent. Leave the fibre wet.

2. Fill the pot with the 10 litres (350 fl oz) of water. The temperature of the water should be 80°C–90°C (175°F–195°F).

3. Combine the indigo powder with 50 ml (1.7 fl oz) of the boiling water in one of the jars or containers and mix them into a paste until all lumps are removed.

4. Combine the calcium hydroxide with 50 ml (1.7 fl oz) of the boiling water in one of the jars or containers and mix until dissolved.

5. Combine the fructose with 50 ml (1.7 fl oz) of the boiling water in one of the jars or containers and mix until wet. It will not completely dissolve.

6. Add the indigo solution to the pot of hot water, then add the calcium hydroxide solution and the fructose solution.

7. Stir the ingredients in the pot gently by creating a vortex. This will prevent too much air getting into the water.

8. Allow the water in the pot to settle for 45 minutes. When the water has cooled there should be some bubbles and a coppery sheen on the surface.

9. If you are planning to use a resist-dyeing technique (see pages 104–113), this should be done now.

10. Using tongs, immerse the fibre in the indigo dye bath for 1–5 minutes then remove it gently. Squeeze any excess liquid back into the pot. Try to avoid the fibre touching the bottom of the vat where there may be some sediment, which can leave unwanted marks.

11. The fibre will be a yellowish colour at this point; it will develop into a blue as it oxidises.

12. Hang the fibre until it turns completely blue, then repeat the dyeing process until you reach your desired depth of shade.

13. Once the entire fibre is blue, rinse it with cold water and a gentle detergent until the water turns clear.

14. If you used any resist-dyeing techniques, remove the rubber bands, string etc. from the fabric.

15. Dry the fabric and iron on an appropriate setting to remove creases.

TECHNIQUES

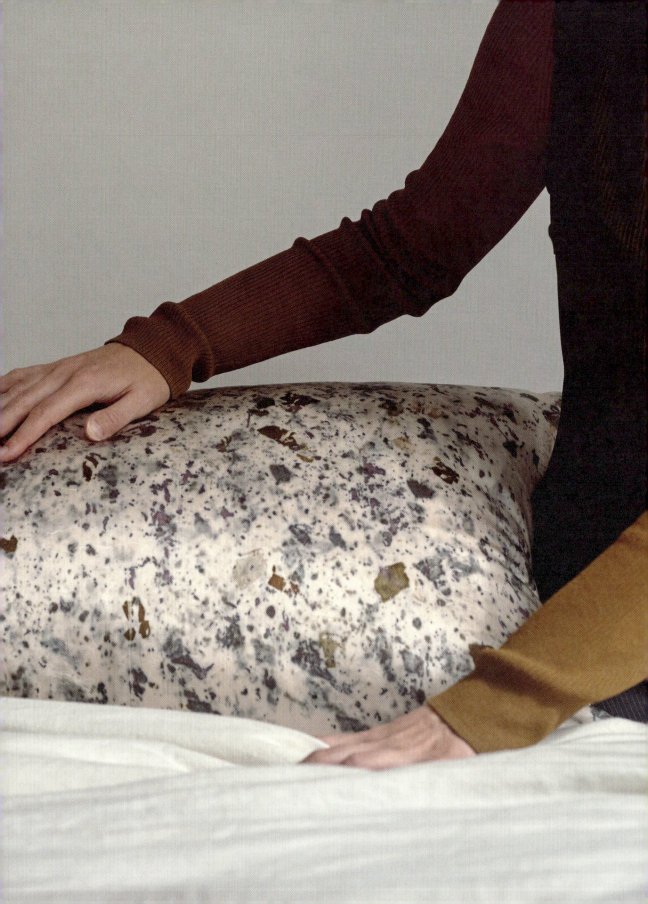

PART 3

Projects

Avocado and onion
skin silk camisole

You will need:

gentle detergent

1 silk camisole

aluminium potassium sulphate 10% WOF

2 stainless steel pots

5 whole avocado stones, fresh or frozen, washed

1 handful brown onion skins

1 handful fresh marigolds

1 wooden dowel or plastic tube

string or rubber bands

1 steamer pot

tongs

Method:

1. Pre-wash the silk camisole in a hot cycle in the washing machine using a gentle detergent.

2. Mordant the camisole with aluminium potassium sulphate in a pot according to the instructions on page 26.

3. Rinse the camisole and set it aside.

4. Make the avocado dye bath by adding the avocado stones to a pot of water large enough for the fabric to move around freely.

5. Bring the dye bath to just below simmering and hold the temperature for 1–2 hours until the water turns a deep, clear pink.

6. Remove the dye bath from the heat and immerse the wet camisole.

7. Allow the camisole to soak for 1–24 hours or until it reaches your desired depth of shade. The longer the fabric is left in the dye bath, the darker the colour will be.

8. Remove the camisole from the pot and rinse it in cold water.

9. Lay the camisole flat on a table.

10. Place the onion skins and marigold petals over the fabric according to the instructions on pages 80–95. You can leave the skins whole or tear or cut them depending on your desired print.

11. Roll the camisole from the bottom up until you end up with a long roll. You can use the wooden dowel or plastic tube for this.

12. Use the string or rubber bands to tie the fabric into a bundle.

13. Using tongs, place the bundle in a steamer pot for 30–45 minutes. Check it from time to time to see if the colour is coming through.

14. Using tongs, remove the bundle from the steamer pot and allow it to cool.

15. Unbundle the camisole and brush off the plant material.

16. At this point, you can use a modifier according to the instructions on pages 37–39. I did not use a modifier for the camisole pictured.

17. Rinse the camisole in cold water using a gentle detergent and hang it to dry. Iron on an appropriate setting to remove creases.

PROJECTS

Substitutes and variants:

Fabric: Any other natural fibre mordanted with an appropriate mordant from pages 24–25.

Dyes: Other plants that create a similar look and colour to onion skins include yellow or orange flowers like marigold, black-eyed Susan, goldenrod, coreopsis and dyer's chamomile, but you can use any other plants you have on hand. Plants that create a similar colour to avocado stones include cutch with a sodium carbonate modifier or madder root.

Mordant: Substitute any other mordant for aluminium potassium sulphate according to the instructions on page 26.

PROJECTS   Easy   147

Hibiscus silk shirt

You will need:

gentle detergent

1 silk shirt

iron 2% WOF

1 stainless steel pot

1 handful fresh hibiscus flowers

1 wooden dowel or plastic tube

string or rubber bands

1 steamer pot

tongs

Method:

1. Pre-wash the silk shirt in a hot cycle in the washing machine using a gentle detergent.
2. Mordant the shirt with iron in a pot according to the instructions on pages 24–25.
3. Rinse the shirt in cold water.
4. Lay the shirt flat on a table.
5. Place the hibiscus flowers on half of the shirt according to the instructions on pages 84–85. You can leave the flowers whole or remove the petals.
6. Roll the shirt from the bottom up until you end up with a long roll. You can use the wooden dowel or plastic tube for this.
7. Use the string or rubber bands to tie the fabric into a bundle.
8. Using tongs, place the bundle in a steamer pot for 30–45 minutes. Check it from time to time to see if the colour is coming through.
9. Using tongs, remove the bundle from the steamer pot and allow it to cool.
10. Unbundle the shirt and brush off the plant material.
11. At this point, you can use a modifier according to the instructions on pages 37–39. I did not use a modifier for the shirt pictured.
12. Rinse the shirt in cold water using a gentle detergent and hang it to dry. Iron on an appropriate setting to remove creases.

Substitutes and variants:

Fabric: Any other natural fibre mordanted with an appropriate mordant from pages 24–25.

Dyes: Other plants that create a similar look and colour to hibiscus flowers include red roses and red geraniums.

Mordant: Substitute any other mordant for ferrous sulphate according to the instructions on page 28.

Rust linen top

You will need:

gentle detergent

1 linen top

cardboard, plastic or a thick piece of fabric

200 ml (7 fl oz) vinegar

200 ml (7 fl oz) cold water

1 spray bottle

rusty objects

dye, ink or extract powder (optional)

1 bowl, container or plastic bag

Method:

1. Pre-wash the linen top in a hot cycle in the washing machine using a gentle detergent.

2. Lay the wet top flat on a table with a protective layer of cardboard, plastic or fabric underneath to avoid staining the surface.

3. Pour the vinegar and the cold water into the spray bottle.

4. Spray the entire garment with the water/vinegar mixture.

5. Lay the rusty objects on top of the fabric and spray them with the water/vinegar mixture.

6. Either leave the objects sitting on top of the fabric, or roll the fabric up with the objects inside. I used some relatively flat pieces of rusty metal, so I layered them between the fabric, making sure that the metal was touching as much of the fabric as possible to avoid too much white space.

7. At this point you can also spray or drip some dye, ink or extract powders over the fabric. Be aware that the dyes will react with the iron oxide and darken in colour. This can create unique and beautiful results.

8. Place the top in the bowl, container or plastic bag and leave for around 24 hours.

9. Unwrap the fabric and put aside the rusty objects for later use.

10. Rinse the top in cold water using a gentle detergent and hang it to dry. Iron on an appropriate setting to remove creases.

Substitutes and variants:

Fabric: Any other pre-washed natural fibre.

Indigo linen robe

You will need:

gentle detergent

1 linen robe

10 litres (350 fl oz) water, just below boiling

1 stainless steel pot

50 g (1.8 oz) indigo powder

100 g (3.5 oz) calcium hydroxide

150 g (5.5 oz) fructose

150 ml (5 fl oz) boiling water

3 jars or containers

rubber bands

tongs

Method:

1. Pre-wash the linen robe in a hot cycle in the washing machine using a gentle detergent. Leave the fabric wet.
2. Fill the pot with the 10 litres (350 fl oz) of water. The temperature of the water should be 80°C–90°C (175°F–195°F).
3. Combine the indigo powder with 50 ml (1.7 fl oz) of the boiling water in one of the jars or containers and mix them into a paste until all lumps are removed.
4. Combine the calcium hydroxide with 50 ml (1.7 fl oz) of the boiling water in one of the jars or containers and mix until dissolved.
5. Combine the fructose with 50 ml (1.7 fl oz) of the boiling water in one of the jars or containers and mix until wet. It will not completely dissolve.
6. Add the indigo solution to the pot of hot water, then add the calcium hydroxide solution and the fructose solution.
7. Stir the ingredients in the pot gently by creating a vortex. This will prevent too much air getting into the water.
8. Allow the water in the pot to settle for 45 minutes. When the water has cooled there should be some bubbles and a coppery sheen on the surface.
9. Tie the robe using rubber bands according to the instructions on page 107.
10. Using tongs, immerse the tied robe in the indigo dye bath for 1–5 minutes then remove it gently. Squeeze any excess liquid back into the pot.
11. The fibre will be a yellowish colour at this point; it will develop into a blue as it oxidises.
12. Hang the robe until it turns completely blue, then repeat the dyeing process until you reach your desired depth of shade.

> **Tip:** The indigo dye bath can be kept and used over and over. When it begins to run out of colour, you can top up the water and add the same ingredients again.

PROJECTS   151

13. Once the entire fibre is blue, rinse it with cold water and a gentle detergent until the water turns clear.
14. Remove the rubber bands from the fabric.
15. Dry the robe and iron on an appropriate setting to remove creases.

Substitutes and variants:

Fabric: Any other pre-washed natural fibre.

Dyes: You can replace indigo with any other dyes you have on hand and mordant accordingly.

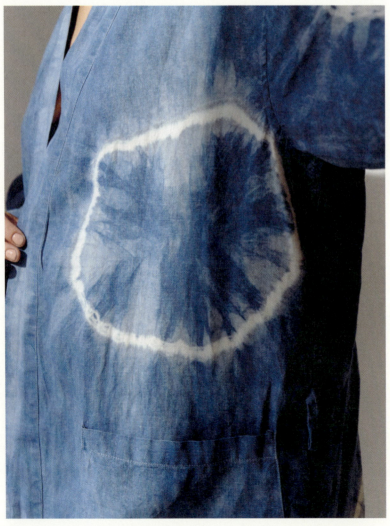

154 Easy   HAND DYED DESIGNS

Bleached linen jacket

You will need:

gentle detergent

1 linen jacket

iron 2% WOF

2 stainless steel pots

tannin 8% WOF

50 ml (1.7 fl oz) lemon juice

50 ml (1.7 fl oz) cold water

Method:

1. Pre-wash the linen jacket in a hot cycle in the washing machine using a gentle detergent.

2. Mordant the jacket with the iron in a pot according to the instructions on page 28.

3. Make a tannin dye bath by dissolving the tannin in a pot of boiling water large enough for the fabric to move around freely. The pot can be taken off the heat once the tannin is mixed in.

4. Immerse the iron-mordanted jacket in the tannin dye bath.

5. Allow the jacket to soak for 30–45 minutes, stirring occasionally.

6. Remove the jacket and rinse it in cold water using a gentle detergent.

7. Hang or machine dry the jacket and iron to remove all creases.

8. Lay the jacket flat on a table.

9. Mix the lemon juice with the cold water to dilute the acid.

10. Use your fingers to flick the lemon water over the jacket. The bleach effect will take place almost immediately and continue developing for around 5 minutes. If you want a stronger effect, don't dilute the acid. Instead, you can simply squeeze the lemon juice directly onto the jacket.

11. Allow the lemon juice to dry completely on the jacket for at least 24 hours.

12. Rinse the jacket in cold water using a gentle detergent and hang it to dry. Iron on an appropriate setting to remove creases.

Substitutes and variants:

Fabric: Any other natural fibre mordanted with an appropriate mordant from pages 24–25.

Dyes: You can replace tannin powder with any other dye high in tannin such as eucalyptus leaves, avocado stones, black tea, cutch, acorns or tara.

Mordant: This recipe requires the use of iron and will not be as effective using another mordant.

PROJECTS

PROJECTS   **Advanced**   157

Striped linen pants

You will need:

gentle detergent

1 pair linen pants

tannin 8% WOF

1 stainless steel pot

2 g (0.07 oz) iron (ferrous sulphate)

80 ml (2.6 fl oz) pre-mixed guar gum solution (see page 117)

30 ml (1 fl oz) hot water

1 jar

thick cardboard

1 large and flat paintbrush

Method:

1. Pre-wash the linen pants in a hot cycle in the washing machine using a gentle detergent. Leave them wet.
2. Make a tannin dye bath by dissolving the tannin powder in a pot of boiling water large enough for the fabric to move around freely. The pot can be taken off the heat once the tannin is mixed in.
3. Immerse the wet pants in the tannin dye bath.
4. Allow the pants to soak for 30–45 minutes, stirring occasionally.
5. Remove the pants from the dye bath, rinse with cold water and allow them to dry completely.
6. Iron the pants to remove all creases.
7. Make the iron paint by combining the iron and the hot water in a jar. Stir until the iron has dissolved. Add the pre-mixed guar gum solution and stir (see page 117).
8. Lay the pants flat on a table or the floor. Place the cardboard inside the legs to prevent the paint from seeping through.
9. Use the paintbrush to paint a pattern of your choice on the front of the pants.
10. Allow the paint to dry completely.
11. Turn the pants over and paint the reverse side.
12. Allow the paint to dry completely.
13. Wash the pants with a gentle detergent and hang them to dry. Iron on an appropriate setting to remove creases.

Substitutes and variants:

Fabric: Any other natural fibre mordanted with an appropriate mordant from pages 24–25.

Dyes: You can replace tannin powder with any other dye high in tannin, such as eucalyptus leaves, avocado stones, black tea, cutch, acorns or tara.

Intermediate   HAND DYED DESIGNS

Soy and cutch linen hat

You will need:

gentle detergent

1 linen hat

50 ml (1.7 fl oz) soy milk

50 ml (1.7 fl oz) pre-mixed guar
gum solution (see page 117)

1 jar

1 large and flat paintbrush

cutch 30% WOF

½ teaspoon sodium carbonate

1 stainless steel pot

Method:

1. Pre-wash the linen hat in a hot cycle in the washing machine using a gentle detergent.

2. Allow the hat to dry completely.

3. Make the soy paint by combining the soy milk and the pre-mixed guar gum solution in the jar. Mix well.

4. Use the paintbrush to paint the dry hat with the soy paint.

5. Allow the paint to dry completely for 24 hours.

6. Make a cutch dye bath by combining the cutch and the sodium carbonate in a pot of boiling water large enough for the fabric to move around freely. The pot can be taken off the heat once the ingredients have been mixed in.

7. Immerse the dry, painted hat in the dye bath and stir until it is completely wet.

8. Allow the hat to soak for up to 2 hours, stirring regularly.

9. Remove the hat from the dye bath.

10. Rinse the hat in cold water using a gentle detergent and hang it to dry. Iron on an appropriate setting to remove creases.

Substitutes and variants:

Fabric: Any other natural fibre mordanted with an appropriate mordant from pages 24–25.

Dyes: Other plants that create a similar look and colour include madder root and black walnut.

Paint: Substitute iron or aluminium paint for soy according to the instructions on page 120.

PROJECTS   Easy   161

Onion skin cotton apron

You will need:

gentle detergent

1 cotton apron

aluminium acetate 8% WOF

calcium carbonate 5% WOF

1 stainless steel pot

1 handful brown onion skins

1 wooden dowel or plastic tube

string or rubber bands

1 steamer pot

tongs

Method:

1. Scour or pre-wash the cotton apron in a hot cycle in the washing machine using a gentle detergent according to instructions on page 18.
2. Mordant the apron in aluminium acetate followed by a calcium carbonate afterbath according to the instructions on page 28.
3. Rinse the apron and wring dry.
4. Lay the apron flat on a table or the floor.
5. Place the onion skins over the fabric according to the instructions on pages 80–95. You can leave the skins whole or tear or cut them depending on your desired print.
6. Roll the apron from the bottom up until you end up with a long roll. You can use the wooden dowel or plastic tube for this. You will notice that the outside is still white. Lay the onion skins along the top before rolling into a bundle (see image on page 85).
7. Use the string or rubber bands to tie the fabric into a bundle.
8. Using tongs, place the bundle in the steamer pot for 30–45 minutes. Check it from time to time to see if the colour is coming through.
9. Using tongs, remove the bundle from the steamer pot and allow it to cool.
10. Unbundle the apron and brush off the onion skins.
11. You can use a modifier according to the instructions on pages 37–38 at this point. I did not use a modifier for the apron pictured.
12. Rinse the apron in cold water using a gentle detergent and hang it to dry. Iron on an appropriate setting to remove creases.

Substitutes and variants:

Fabric: Any other natural fibre mordanted with an appropriate mordant from pages 24–25.

Dyes: Other plants that create a similar look and colour include yellow or orange flowers like marigold, black-eyed Susan, goldenrod, coreopsis and dyer's chamomile, but you can use any other plants you have on hand. Red onion skins will produce more brown/green shades.

Mordant: Substitute any other mordant for aluminium acetate according to the instructions on page 28.

Madder and marigold socks

You will need:

gentle detergent

1 pair cotton socks

aluminium acetate 8% WOF

calcium carbonate 5% WOF

1 stainless steel pot

madder powder

marigold powder

pomegranate extract

1 wooden dowel or plastic tube

string or rubber bands

1 steamer pot

tongs

Method:

1. Scour or pre-wash the cotton socks in a hot cycle in the washing machine using a gentle detergent.
2. Mordant the socks in aluminium acetate followed by a calcium carbonate afterbath according to the instructions on page 28.
3. Rinse the socks and wring dry.
4. Lay the socks flat on a table or the floor.
5. Sprinkle the madder powder, marigold powder and pomegranate extract over one side of the socks. Flip the socks over and repeat on the other side.
6. Roll the socks according to the instructions on page 84. You can use the wooden dowel or plastic tube for this.
7. Use the string or rubber bands to tie the socks into a bundle.
8. Using tongs, place the bundle in the steamer pot for 30–45 minutes. Check it from time to time to see if the colour is coming through.
9. Using tongs, remove the bundle from the steamer pot and allow it to cool.
10. Unbundle the socks and rinse off the powders.
11. At this point you can use a modifier according to the instructions on pages 37–38. I did not use a modifier for the socks pictured.
12. Rinse the socks in cold water using a gentle detergent and hang them to dry. Iron on an appropriate setting to remove creases.

Substitutes and variants:

Fabric: Any other natural fibre mordanted with an appropriate mordant from pages 24–25.

Dyes: Any other dye powder or extract to create a similar speckled print.

Mordant: Substitute any other mordant for aluminium acetate according to the instructions on page 28.

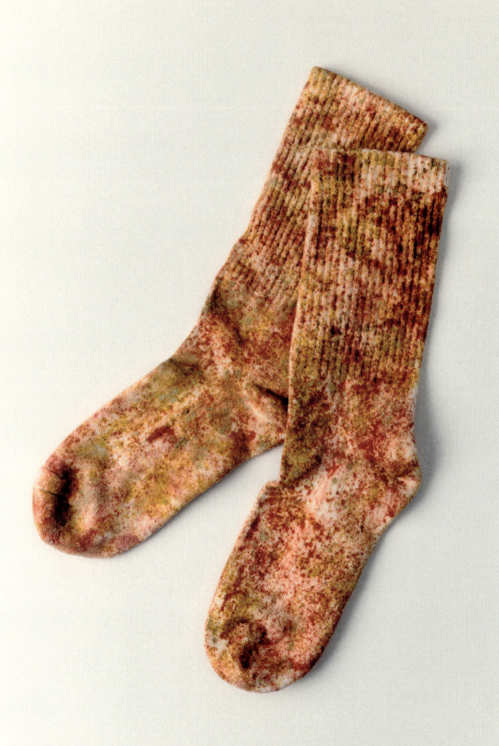

PROJECTS   Advanced   165

Handpainted linen top

You will need:

gentle detergent

1 linen top

aluminium acetate 8% WOF

calcium carbonate 5% WOF

1 stainless steel pot

thick cardboard

1 teaspoon logwood extract

1 teaspoon fustic extract

1 teaspoon cutch extract

150 ml (5 fl oz) boiling water

3 jars

3 large and flat paintbrushes

Method:

1. Pre-wash the top in a hot cycle in the washing machine using a gentle detergent.

2. Mordant the top in aluminium acetate followed by a calcium carbonate afterbath in a pot according to the instructions on page 28.

3. Rinse the top and wring dry.

4. Lay the wet top on a flat surface.

5. Place the cardboard between the layers of the garment to prevent the inks from seeping through.

6. Combine the logwood extract with 50 ml (1.7 fl oz) of the boiling water in one of the jars.

7. Combine the fustic extract with 50 ml (1.7 fl oz) of the boiling water in one of the jars.

8. Combine the cutch extract with 50 ml (1.7 fl oz) of the boiling water in one of the jars.

9. Use a large flat paintbrush (one paintbrush per dye) to apply the dye to the top in diagonal stripes.

10. Dry the paint. When the paint on both sides is completely dry, rinse the top thoroughly in cold water until the water runs clear.

11. Heat set the inks using either a dryer, iron or steamer (see page 127).

12. If you have the time, this technique benefits from 1–2 weeks (or more) of curing before washing again with detergent.

13. Wash the fabric thoroughly with a gentle detergent. Allow it to dry and iron if necessary.

Substitutes and variants:

Fabric: Any other natural fibre mordanted with an appropriate mordant from pages 24–25.

Dyes: Any other ink using an extract, powder or whole plant according to the instructions on pages 126–130.

Mordant: Substitute any other mordant for aluminium acetate according to the instructions on page 28.

166 Intermediate · HAND DYED DESIGNS

Soy and black tea dress

You will need:

gentle detergent

1 cotton dress

thick cardboard

50 ml (1.7 fl oz) soy milk (store-bought or home-made, without additives such as oil)

50 ml (1.7 fl oz) pre-mixed guar gum solution (optional) (see page 117)

1 jar

1 paintbrush

1 stainless steel pot

black tea 100% WOF

tongs

Method:

1. Scour or pre-wash the cotton dress in a hot cycle in the washing machine using a gentle detergent.

2. Allow the dress to dry completely. Iron it to remove all creases.

3. Lay the dress flat on a table or the floor.

4. Place the cardboard between the two layers of the dress to avoid the paint seeping through.

5. Either use soy milk on its own or make a soy paint by combining the soy milk and the pre-mixed guar gum solution in the jar. Mix well.

6. Use the paintbrush to apply the soy paint to the dress in your desired design.

7. Allow the paint to dry completely over 24 hours.

8. Make a black tea bath by soaking tea leaves (or bags) in a pot of water large enough for the fabric to move around freely. Bring to the boil for 15–30 minutes then strain the leaves out if necessary.

9. Using tongs, immerse the soy-painted dress in the tea dye bath and allow it to soak for at least 1 hour, stirring regularly.

10. Remove the dress from the dye bath, rinse in cold water using a gentle detergent and hang it to dry. Iron on an appropriate setting to remove creases.

Substitutes and variants:

Fabric: Any other pre-washed natural fibre.

Dyes: Any other dye tannin such as cutch, walnut or avocado. Clear tannins like tara, myrobalan and oak galls will not work with this recipe unless you use an iron paint instead.

Mordant: Substitute any other mordant paint for soy milk according to the instructions on page 120.

Two-tone silk pillowcases

You will need:

gentle detergent

2 silk pillowcases

rubber bands

cutch extract 20% WOF

10 litres (350 fl oz) water, just below boiling

2 stainless steel pots

50 g (1.8 oz) indigo powder

100 g (3.5 oz) calcium hydroxide

150 g (5.5 oz) fructose

150 ml (5 fl oz) boiling water

3 jars or containers

tongs

Method:

1. Pre-wash the silk pillowcases in a hot cycle in the washing machine using a gentle detergent.

2. While still wet, tie a rubber band tightly around the end of each pillowcase.

3. Create a cutch dye bath by dissolving the cutch extract in a small amount of boiling water and adding it to a pot of warm or cold water (see pages 70–79).

4. Place one end of each pillowcase in the cutch dye bath and allow them to soak for around 15 minutes.

5. Fill the other pot with the 10 litres (350 fl oz) of water. The temperature of the water should be 80°C–90°C (175°F–195°F).

6. Combine the indigo with 50 ml (1.7 fl oz) of the boiling water in one of the jars or containers and mix them into a paste until all lumps are removed.

7. Combine the calcium hydroxide with 50 ml (1.7 fl oz) of the boiling water in one of the jars or containers and mix until dissolved.

8. Combine the fructose with 50 ml (1.7 fl oz) of the boiling water in one of the jars or containers and mix until wet. It will not completely dissolve.

9. Add the indigo solution to the pot of hot water, then add the calcium hydroxide solution and the fructose solution.

10. Stir the ingredients in the pot gently by creating a vortex. This will prevent too much air getting into the water.

11. Allow the water in the pot to settle for 45 minutes. When the water has cooled, there should be some bubbles and a coppery sheen on the surface.

12. Using tongs, immerse the undyed ends of the pillowcases in the indigo dye for 1–5 minutes.

13. Remove the pillowcases from the dye. The fibre will be a yellowish colour at this point; it will develop into a blue as it oxidises.

14. Continue to build the colour by dipping the pillowcases multiple times until you reach your desired depth of shade.

15. Once the depth of shade is to your liking, rinse the pillowcases in cold water to remove any excess dye.

16. Hang the pillowcases to dry. Iron on an appropriate setting to remove creases.

PROJECTS

Substitutes and variants:

Fabric: Any other pre-washed natural fibre.

Dyes: Any other natural dyes in immersion dye baths according to the instructions on pages 70–79.

Mordant: Although no mordant is required for this recipe, if you choose alternative dyes to indigo and cutch, you can mordant the fabric using an appropriate mordant from pages 24–25.

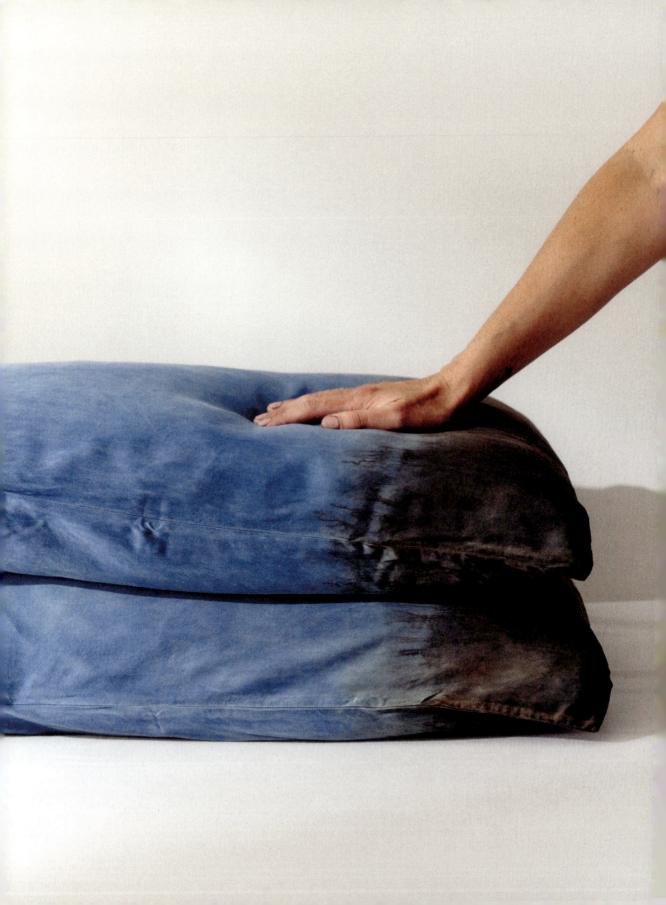

PROJECTS

PROJECTS   Intermediate   173

Flower-printed cotton bag

You will need:

gentle detergent

1 cotton bag

iron 2% WOF

1 stainless steel pot

red rose petals

string or rubber bands

1 steamer pot

tongs

Method:

1. Scour or pre-wash the cotton bag in a hot cycle in the washing machine using a gentle detergent.

2. Mordant the bag with iron in a pot according to the instructions on page 28.

3. Lay the wet cotton bag on a flat surface and place the rose petals on the fabric according to the instructions on pages 80–95.

4. Roll the fabric into a bundle.

5. Use the string or rubber bands to tie the bundle tightly.

6. Using tongs, place the bundle in a steamer pot for 30 minutes, then remove it and allow to cool.

7. Unwrap the bundle, rinse in cold water with a gentle detergent and hang to dry. Iron to remove creases if necessary.

Substitutes and variants:

Fabric: Any other natural fibre mordanted with an appropriate mordant on pages 24–25.

Dyes: Other flowers that create a similar colour include red geraniums and red hibiscus.

Mordant: Iron can be substituted with another mordant on page 28.

Ink tie-dyed silk sarong

You will need:

gentle detergent

1 silk sarong

aluminium potassium sulphate
10%–15% WOF

1 stainless steel pot

1 teaspoon logwood extract

1 teaspoon cutch extract

1 teaspoon marigold extract

1 teaspoon fustic extract

200 ml (7 fl oz) hot water

4 jars

rubber bands

1 steamer pot

tongs

Method:

1. Pre-wash the silk sarong in a hot cycle in the washing machine using a gentle detergent.

2. Mordant the sarong with aluminium potassium sulphate in a pot according to the instructions on page 26.

3. Combine the logwood extract with 50 ml (1.7 fl oz) of the boiling water in one of the jars. Stir until completely dissolved.

4. Combine the cutch extract with 50 ml (1.7 fl oz) of the boiling water in one of the jars. Stir until completely dissolved.

5. Combine the marigold extract with 50 ml (1.7 fl oz) of the boiling water in one of the jars. Stir until completely dissolved.

6. Combine the fustic with 50 ml (1.7 fl oz) of the boiling water in one of the jars. Stir until completely dissolved.

7. Lay the sarong flat on a table. Begin scrunching the fabric into the centre according to the image on page 106.

8. Once you have a scrunched ball, secure it lightly with the rubber bands.

9. Pour, spray or drip the inks over one side of the bundled sarong.

10. Turn the bundle over and do the same on the opposite side. You should use sufficient ink to completely cover the sarong and allow it to absorb the colour, but ensure not to use so much that it is dripping ink.

11. Using tongs, place the sarong in the steamer pot for 45–60 minutes.

12. Using tongs, remove the fabric from the steamer pot and allow it to cool.

13. Untie the rubber bands and rinse the sarong in cold water using a gentle detergent.

14. Allow the sarong to dry and iron to remove creases if necessary.

PROJECTS

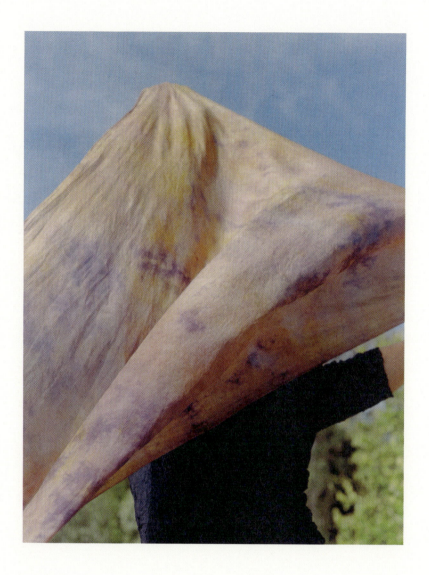

Substitutes and variants:

Fabric: Any other natural fibre mordanted with an appropriate mordant from pages 24–25.

Dyes: You can replace the dyes with any other natural dyes. If you are not using extracts, follow instead the raw plant dye ink recipe on page 130. A binder is not necessary for this recipe.

Mordant: Substitute any other mordant for aluminium potassium sulphate according to the instructions on page 26.

PROJECTS

Easy 179

Marigold velvet cushion cover

You will need:

gentle detergent

1 velvet cushion cover

iron 2% WOF

1 stainless steel pot

marigold powder 20%–30% WOF
or whole flowers 100% WOF

1 strainer

tongs

Method:

1. Pre-wash the velvet cushion cover in a hot cycle in the washing machine using a gentle detergent.

2. Mordant the cushion cover with iron in a pot according to the instructions on page 28.

3. Rinse the cushion cover and wring dry.

4. Make a marigold dye bath using either the powder or whole flowers according to the instructions on pages 70–79. Remember that the process is slightly different for powders and whole plants, but either dye will need to be strained before use.

5. Using tongs, immerse the cushion cover in the dye bath and allow it to soak for 45–60 minutes, stirring regularly.

6. Rinse the cushion cover in cold water using a gentle detergent and hang it to dry. Iron on an appropriate setting to remove creases.

Substitutes and variants:

Fabric: Any other natural fibre mordanted with an appropriate mordant from pages 24–25.

Dyes: Other plants that create a similar green with ferrous sulphate include yellow or orange flowers like marigold, black-eyed Susan, goldenrod, coreopsis and dyer's chamomile, and brown or red onion skins, but you can use any other plants to make an alternative colour.

Mordant: Substitute any other mordant for iron according to the instructions on page 28.

Cutch and iron silk top

You will need:

gentle detergent

1 silk top

cutch 20% WOF

2 stainless steel pots

rubber bands

iron 2% WOF

tongs

Method:

1. Pre-wash the silk top in a hot cycle in the washing machine using a gentle detergent. Leave the top wet.

2. Create a cutch dye bath by dissolving the cutch extract in a small amount of boiling water and adding it to a pot of warm or cold water (see pages 70–79).

3. Immerse the wet top in the cutch dye bath and allow it to soak for 30–60 minutes, stirring regularly.

4. Remove the top from the dye bath and rinse in cold water.

5. Lay the top on a flat surface and tie loosely according to instructions on page 107. Ensure the rubber bands are tied tightly.

6. Make an iron modifier bath in a pot by adding the iron to hot tap water. Stir until the iron is completely dissolved (see page 37).

7. Using tongs, immerse the top in the iron modifier bath for 2–5 minutes.

8. Using tongs, remove the top from the modifier bath and rinse under cold water with the rubber bands still attached.

9. Remove the rubber bands and rinse the top again in cold water using a gentle detergent. Hang it to dry then iron on an appropriate setting to remove creases.

Substitutes and variants:

Fabric: Any other natural fibre mordanted with an appropriate mordant from pages 24–25.

Dyes: Any other dye plant in an immersion dye bath according to the instructions on pages 70–79.

Modifier: Any other modifier according to the instructions on pages 37–38.

PROJECTS   Easy   183

Logwood sprinkled t-shirt

You will need:

gentle detergent

1 cotton t-shirt

aluminium acetate 8% WOF

calcium carbonate 5% WOF

1 stainless steel pot

rubber gloves

logwood extract

string or rubber bands

1 steamer pot

tongs

Method:

1. Scour or pre-wash the cotton t-shirt in a hot cycle in the washing machine using a gentle detergent.

2. Mordant the t-shirt in aluminium acetate followed by a calcium carbonate afterbath in a pot according to the instructions on page 28.

3. Rinse the t-shirt and wring dry.

4. Lay the t-shirt on a flat surface.

5. Wearing gloves, sprinkle the logwood extract over the top of the damp t-shirt.

6. Turn the t-shirt over and repeat on the reverse side. Leave it to sit for 10 minutes.

7. Roll the t-shirt gently into a bundle and tie it with the string or rubber bands. It is not necessary to secure the rubber bands or string tightly.

8. Using tongs, place the bundle in a steamer pot and steam for 30–45 minutes.

9. Using tongs, remove the bundle from the steamer pot and allow it to cool.

10. Unbundle the t-shirt.

11. At this point, you can use a modifier according to the instructions on pages 37–38. I did not use a modifier for the t-shirt pictured.

12. Rinse the t-shirt in cold water using a gentle detergent and hang it to dry. Iron on an appropriate setting to remove creases.

Substitutes and variants:

Fabric: Any other natural fibre mordanted with an appropriate mordant from pages 24–25.

Dyes: Any other dye powder or extract to create a similar speckled print.

Mordant: Substitute any other mordant for aluminium acetate according to the instructions on page 28.

Pomegranate and geranium
silk eye mask

You will need:

gentle detergent

1 silk eye mask

iron 2% WOF

2 stainless steel pots

1–2 pomegranate rinds
(seeds removed)

1 handful red geranium flowers

string or rubber bands

1 steamer pot

tongs

Method:

1. Pre-wash the silk eye mask in a hot cycle in the washing machine using a gentle detergent.

2. Mordant the eye mask in iron in a pot according to the instructions on page 28.

3. Rinse the eye mask and wring dry.

4. Make a pomegranate dye bath by bringing a pot of water to a simmer and adding the pomegranate rinds. Simmer for at least 60 minutes until the pigment begins to show, then remove the pot from the heat and strain the dye (see pages 70–79).

5. Immerse the eye mask in the dye bath for 30–60 minutes.

6. Remove the eye mask from the dye bath, rinse in cold water and lay on a flat surface.

7. Sprinkle the red geranium petals over the top of the eye mask.

8. Roll the fabric into a bundle according to the instructions on pages 80–95.

9. Tie the bundle with the string or rubber bands.

10. Using tongs, place the bundle in the steamer pot for 30–45 minutes. Check it from time to time to see if the colour is coming through.

11. Using tongs, remove the bundle from the steamer pot and allow it to cool.

12. Unbundle the eye mask and brush off the flowers.

13. Rinse the eye mask in cold water using a gentle detergent and hang it to dry. Iron on an appropriate setting to remove creases.

Substitutes and variants:

Fabric: Any other natural fibre mordanted with an appropriate mordant from pages 24–25.

Dyes: Other plants that create a similar colour and print to geraniums include other red flowers like red roses or hibiscus. Other plants that create a similar colour to pomegranate are marigold powder or onion skins (red or brown).

Mordant: Substitute any other mordant for ferrous sulphate according to the instructions on page 28.

PART 4

Textile Care and Sustainability

Washing hand-dyed textiles

Like all well-used textiles, naturally dyed textiles may fade slightly over time as they are used and loved. To keep colours bright, I recommend handwashing with cold water using a gentle natural detergent. If you must machine wash your items, use a cold, delicate wash. Hang them to dry in the shade. Use an iron on the setting appropriate for the fabric.

Many big brand detergents use harsh chemicals that can fade natural dyes. For this reason, don't use bleach or stain removers and choose a plant-based, natural detergent. Most detergents are slightly alkaline, which means that your colours may change slightly when you wash them if your dye bath is at a lower pH. I don't worry about this too much; the changes are generally minimal. Check with your laundry detergent manufacturer to see what the pH of their product is. My detergent has a pH of just above 8 and I don't notice any colour changes, but if yours has a higher pH, it might be best to find an alternative. In the absence of an appropriate detergent, you can use hand soap or shampoo to wash hand-dyed textiles.

Spills and stains

Since natural dyes are pH-sensitive, it's common to notice visible reactions with everyday substances such as bodily fluids, foods or drinks. For example, you may notice stains in the underarm area of your shirt, or if you are cooking and lemon juice sprays onto your clothes, you may notice a colour change. To avoid this, rinse the fabric as soon as possible, using a gentle detergent as specified above. Most colour changes can be minimised or reversed.

Reusing a dye bath

Many dye baths, especially those with a strong pigment, can be used over and over again to create lighter shades. After you have dyed your fibre, check to see if the dye bath has any remaining pigment. If it does, you can dye another item in the same dye bath or use the instructions on pages 132–133 to make a lake pigment. If there is no pigment left, your dye bath has been exhausted and you can dispose of it using the methods below.

Disposing of dyes and mordants

– **Dye bath and tannin:** A dye bath typically only contains plant materials and water, so it is easy to dispose of. If a dye bath has been exhausted of pigment, simply pour it down the drain. Once it has cooled it can also be used to water your garden.

– **Dye plants post-extraction/bundle-dyeing:** If you have a home compost, you can put any used dye plants in it. If not, you can either scatter them throughout your garden or put them into landfill. Some dye plants can also be used again to create an additional dye bath of a lighter shade.

– **Aluminium mordants:** When you use the correct quantities of aluminium, there should be very little left in the water after mordanting your fibres. You can dispose of a spent aluminium bath by digging a small hole in the garden and pouring the contents of the bath inside. Since aluminium is commonly used to reduce pH in soil for acid-loving plants, you can also pour the solution over appropriate plants in your garden. Alternatively, you can keep the water and add more aluminium to make another mordant bath later.

– **Iron:** Iron can be disposed of by either pouring the contents of the bath down the sink, into a hole in the garden, or over acid-loving plants. It is considered a soil acidifier for plants and can even be found in garden stores.

Sustainability

Compared to modern commercial dyeing, natural dyeing at home is inherently kinder to the environment as it doesn't involve the heavy use of toxic chemicals that inevitably end up in waterways, oceans and soils. In saying that, natural dyeing can be energy- and water-intensive if we're not careful. There are a number of ways we can reduce our impact by considering our use of fibres, water, electricity, gas and dyes.

FIBRES

Natural fibres are generally more sustainable than synthetic fibres, since they are made from renewable resources and not from petrochemicals. Yet, there are some natural fibres that are more environmentally friendly than others. Hemp, for example, is on many levels one of the most sustainable plant fibres. It requires significantly less water and land compared to cotton, and can produce large outputs in a short amount of time and with very few herbicides and pesticides. Bamboo grows as quickly as cotton and with far less water; however, the manufacturing stage often involves a highly intensive chemical process. Organic cotton is slightly better than ordinary cotton in that it doesn't involve the heavy use of chemicals; however, it does still use a large amount of water and land. If you don't require a new fibre for your dyeing project, the most sustainable fibre is one that already exists, so see what you can find second-hand. Alternatively, do some research on your chosen fabric to weigh up the pros and cons and make an informed choice.

WATER

Natural dyeing can be water-intensive if you don't take care to limit and reuse your water. If we use fresh water during each step (scouring, mordanting, dyeing and washing), it's easy to use more than 50 litres (13 gallons) for one t-shirt. Here are a few ways you can save water when dyeing at home:

- Reuse your mordant bath. If possible, dedicate a pot for mordanting alone and refill with water when necessary. Recharge the bath with 50% of the usual required mordant (i.e., if you would usually use 10% WOF, use 5% in your reused mordant bath).

- Allow your dye baths and mordant baths to cool and pour over your garden to water your plants.

- Many dye baths still contain a lot of pigment even after you have dyed your chosen fibre. Reuse your dye bath by simply adding more of the same (or different) dye to create a slightly different colour.

- Collect rainwater in a bucket or tank to use for dyeing.

- Rather than using running water for washing and rinsing, fill a bucket that can be used for multiple washes.

ENERGY

While some plants (like eucalyptus leaves) require a long time in hot or boiling water, others can be used with cold or warm water. As discussed on page 79, in the absence of heat we can use time instead. This means that if you have the patience, you can reduce your energy use by allowing your fibres to soak for longer in a cold dye or mordant bath. Keeping a lid on can also trap the heat, which will allow you to turn off the stove earlier and allow the fabric to soak. If you have an outdoor area or are using an open fire for heating purposes, it's also possible to use this heat for dyeing at the same time.

DYES

Any dye that is harvested responsibly from your local area (or your kitchen) is the most sustainable dye you can use, particularly if they are by-products or waste. These include dyes like avocado stones, onion skins, flowers, leaves and acorns. When taking from a living plant, make sure to only take a small amount so the health of the plant isn't affected. When it comes to store-bought natural dyes in extract or powder form, it's more difficult to know where and how they were harvested, and whether sustainable practices were used. If you're unsure, contact the seller to ask for more details like where the dye came from and how it was grown. Regardless of whether your dyes are foraged or purchased, they are all compostable and will break down like any other plant if they are scattered over your garden or in a home compost.

TEXTILE CARE AND SUSTAINABILITY

197

Glossary

Afterbath

An afterbath is a solution of water mixed with a modifier like iron (ferrous sulphate), vinegar or sodium carbonate. The purpose of this solution is to shift the colour of a pre-dyed textile using the chemical reactions that occur when changing the pH and/or adding a metal salt.

Aluminium

Aluminium is the most commonly used mordant for natural dyeing. There are multiple types of aluminium used in natural dyeing, including aluminium acetate, aluminium sulphate and aluminium potassium sulphate. All types of aluminium mordants are 'neutral', meaning that they will not change the colour of the dye. Their purpose is to make natural dyes washfast and lightfast.

Binder

The term binder is used in two circumstances when using natural pigments. Firstly, it is used to describe the way that soy milk is used to treat plant fibres in order to make them more washfast and lightfast. The proteins in soy milk mimic those in animal fibres like silk and wool, which have an affinity for natural dyes. Soy used this way also deepens colours and works similarly to a mordant. Secondly, a binder is a term used when making paint or ink using natural colours. When creating these solutions to paint on fabric, we often mix a gum like gum arabic or guar gum or another binder like honey or egg yolk with the natural pigments. The binder is used to blend with a dry pigment to make paint, or to thicken an ink.

Bundle-dyeing

Also known as eco-printing, bundle-dyeing is a process where natural materials are laid over the fibre, and steam or hot water is used to imprint their shapes and colours permanently onto the fabric. Bundle-dyeing results can be very clear images, or more abstract, where colours and shapes are not necessarily identifiable.

Cellulose fibre

Also known as plant fibres, cellulose fibres are any fibres made from plants, including cotton, hemp, bamboo, linen and other more processed fibres like rayon and lyocell. Cellulose fibres are generally more difficult to dye with natural dyes, as they do not take up or hold the colours as easily as animal fibres. In order to dye cellulose fibres, it is always necessary to use a mordant or soy binder.

Contamination

The term contamination is used to describe what happens when certain substances come in contact with materials or textiles and cause unwanted marks. This is a common occurrence after the use of iron mordants if dyeing using equipment and workspaces that have not been properly cleaned. A dyed piece of fabric can react with the iron, resulting in dark spots. To avoid contamination, it is essential to clean the workspace of any modifiers or mordants that could change the colour of dyed textiles.

Copper

Copper sulphate is a metal salt and mordant that can also affect the colour of some natural dyes, turning them more green or brown. Generally, copper is used after dyeing as a modifier, but it can also be used before dyeing as a mordant. It is a less common mordant than aluminium and iron due to its potential toxicity and the difficulty in disposing of it. A copper pot can be used as a substitute for copper sulphate and can have the same colour-changing effects.

Cream of tartar

Cream of tartar is a by-product of winemaking and can be used in natural dyeing to soften wool or to slightly acidify a dye bath. It is commonly used at 5% WOF in addition to aluminium during the mordanting of wool. In this situation we would call cream of tartar a 'mordant assistant'.

Curing

In the same way that food can be cured for preservation purposes, we can cure our dyes for days or weeks prior to washing in order to allow the pigments to bond more strongly to the fibre and increase colourfastness. Curing for 1–2 weeks is generally suggested, but any delay between the application of the dye and washing the fibre with soap can assist with colourfastness.

Discharge

The term discharge is used in natural dyeing to describe using citric acid to remove or 'discharge' the effect of a metal mordant to part of the fabric in order to create contrast. In the area where the acid has been applied, the mordant is no longer effective, and instead creates a lighter contrast. The effect of this process is particularly noticeable when discharging an iron mordant.

Ferrous sulphate

Ferrous sulphate, also known as iron, is a mordant used in natural dyeing. It is used to increase washfastness and lightfastness, but also has the ability to darken colours. Colours that are ordinarily yellows, browns, oranges, reds and pinks can be transformed into greens, dark browns, greys, purples, blues and sometimes even blacks through the use of ferrous sulphate. This process is known as 'modifying' a natural dye.

Ink

A natural ink is made from a very concentrated natural dye combined with a binding agent like gum arabic, which thickens the solution. Like a dye, but unlike a paint, the pigment in an ink is water-soluble. Inks can also be used on paper, wood, leather and canvas. Their colourfastness is improved by the use of a mordant prior to application.

Lightfast

A lightfast dye is one that can withstand exposure to sunlight without fading dramatically. All dyes will fade with time and use, but some are more resistant than others.

Modifier

When an alkaline, acid or metal mordant is added to a dye bath, the colour of the dye can be changed. These substances are called 'modifiers'. An acidic modifier usually brightens and lightens colours or makes them more yellow. An alkaline modifier generally 'reddens' colours but can sometimes change them to purples to greens. A copper modifier will generally make colours more green or brown. An iron modifier often 'saddens' colours, making them darker. Each plant has a different response to a modifier.

Mordant

A mordant is a substance used to improve the washfastness and lightfastness of natural dyes. Without a mordant, most natural dyes will fade or wash out with time and use. Although a mordant is not always essential with certain combinations of dye and fibre, using one will always improve colourfastness. It is recommended to use a mordant for any dyeing that you want to last well. Some common mordants include aluminium and iron. Copper and tin are more difficult to dispose of and are less popular in modern natural dyeing.

Mordant assistant

A mordant assistant is a substance used to assist in the effectiveness of a mordant. Cream of tartar and sodium carbonate are both examples of mordant assistants. They are not essential, but can help produce the best results.

Protein fibre

A protein fibre, also known as an animal fibre, is made from animal hair like wool from sheep or alpaca, or insect fibres like silk. These fibres contain proteins that cause them to pick up plant dyes more easily than cellulose fibres. For this reason, protein fibres are recommended for beginners, who may want to skip mordanting when they are learning.

GLOSSARY

Resist-dyeing

Resist-dyeing is a technique that allows us to create specific patterns by using materials such as thread, string, plastic, paste, wax or wood to prevent the dye from reaching all parts of the fabric. Tie-dye is an example of resist dyeing. These techniques can create repeated patterns like swirls, circles, stripes and squares in two or more colours.

Scouring

Scouring is a process that involves boiling fibres with detergent and sodium carbonate in order to remove any gums, waxes or oils that may prevent dyes from bonding with the fibre. This process is necessary for plant fibres and fibres that have been previously used. Although dyeing can be successful without this step, scouring will improve the longevity of colours.

Sodium bicarbonate

Also known as baking soda, sodium bicarbonate is an alkali with a pH of around 8. In natural dyeing, sodium bicarbonate can be used as a modifier that is similar to sodium carbonate but slightly weaker.

Sodium carbonate

Sodium carbonate is also known as soda ash or washing soda and is commonly used as an ingredient in cleaning products and soaps. Sodium carbonate has a pH of 11 and will create an alkaline solution when mixed into water or dye. In natural dyeing this ingredient is used as a modifier either in a dye bath or an afterbath in order to change the colour of dye. Sodium carbonate is also used to scour fibres in order to remove gums, waxes and oils that may prevent the pigments from bonding with the fibre.

Tannin

Tannins are naturally occurring molecules found in bark, wood, leaves, roots, fruits, seeds and plant galls. They are commonly used in natural dyeing as mordants for plant fibres. Tannin can be used on its own as a mordant for plant fibres like cotton or linen, or prior to mordanting with aluminium, which is what I recommend for the best results. It can be found in many dye plants such as avocado stones, pomegranate rinds or acorns, or it can be purchased in a powdered dye extract, which is usually made from oak galls. Some tannins are clear and don't colour the fabric, whereas some will dye the fabric light shades of brown or yellow. Tannin is a good option for those who prefer not to use metal salts like aluminium or iron.

Vinegar

White vinegar is used as an acid in natural dyeing to brighten colours or to prevent the dye and mordant in a paint from bonding prior to application to the fabric.

Washfast

A washfast dye is one that can withstand handwashing or machine-washing without significantly fading. All dyes will fade with time and use, but some are more resistant than others.

Weight of fibre (WOF)

Weight of fibre is the term used in natural dyeing to help determine how much dye or mordant to use per gram (ounce) of fibre. It is a helpful way to make sure that the dye bath is strong enough. It can also ensure that there is adequate mordant to treat the fibre, and that there isn't excess left in the water post-mordanting.

About the Author

Katie Ellen Wilkins is an artist based in New South Wales. Born in the USA, she grew up on Boon Wurrung land on the Mornington Peninsula, Victoria and now lives with her husband and two children in Muloobinba/Newcastle. She is the founder of natural dye studio, Studio Tinta, and since 2018 has produced hand-dyed textiles and taught natural dyeing to students around the world. She now hosts natural dyeing and paint-making workshops around Australia. Studio Tinta sells a range of natural dyeing ingredients including dyes and mordants.

Instagram: @ studiotinta_ @ katieellenwilkins_

Web: studiotinta.com.au

ABOUT THE AUTHOR

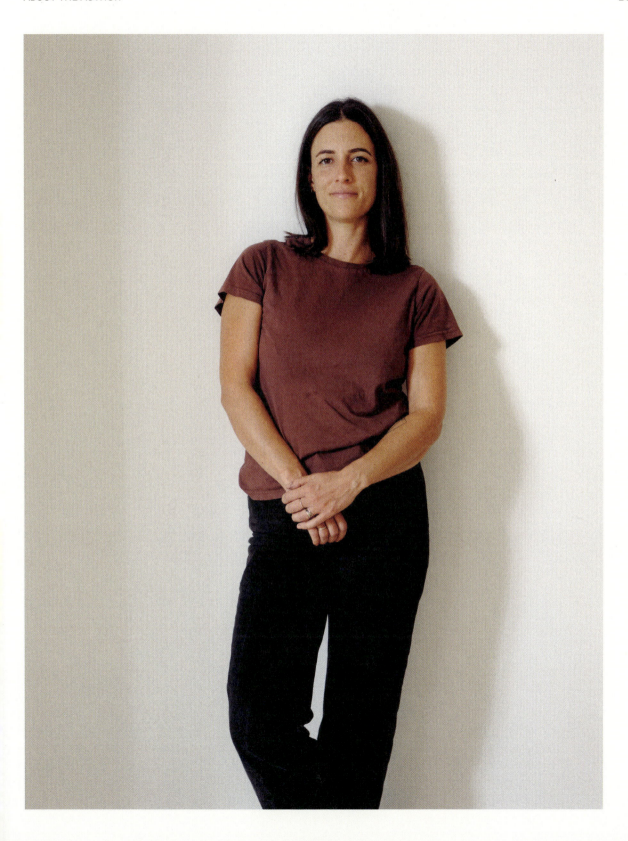

Acknowledgements

The first person I'd like to thank is my beautiful husband and best friend, Johnny. Thank you for encouraging my creative pursuits since day one, and for holding down the fort while I wrote this book. I'm incredibly grateful for your love, support and partnership in this life.

Thank you to my brother Nick who has taken incredible photos for me over the past six years. Without your artistry and talent my work would not have been the same. Thank you to my sister-in-law Marijne for your styling expertise on shoots, advice, occasional modelling and friendship.

To my parents, Sue and John; you have not only offered me your undying support but also many tireless hours of babysitting, especially over summer while I finished this book. My children and I are so lucky to have you in our lives.

To Sandy and Pete for being such beautiful grandparents and friends to our kids and giving Johnny and I the time to pursue our careers. They adore you and so do we.

Thank you to Fiona Hardie and Alice Hardie-Grant who first saw promise in this book, and the rest of the team at Hardie Grant who have helped me through the challenge of writing my first book.

Published in 2025 by Hardie Grant Books, an imprint of Hardie Grant Publishing

Hardie Grant Books (Melbourne)

Wurundjeri Country
Building 1, 658 Church Street
Richmond, Victoria 3121

Hardie Grant North America
2912 Telegraph Ave
Berkeley, California 94705

hardiegrant.com/books

Hardie Grant acknowledges the Traditional Owners of the Country on which we work, the Wurundjeri People of the Kulin Nation and the Gadigal People of the Eora Nation, and recognises their continuing connection to the land, waters and culture. We pay our respects to their Elders past and present.

All rights reserved. No part of this publication may be reproduced, stored in a retrieval system or transmitted in any form by any means, electronic, mechanical, photocopying, recording or otherwise, without the prior written permission of the publishers and copyright holders.

The moral rights of the author have been asserted.

Copyright text © Katie Ellen Wilkins 2025
Copyright photography © Nicholas Wilkins 2025
Copyright design © Hardie Grant Publishing 2025

A catalogue record for this book is available from the National Library of Australia

Hand Dyed Designs: A Guide to Dyeing Textiles with Plants
ISBN: 978 1 76145 036 5
10 9 8 7 6 5 4 3 2 1

Publishers: Alice Hardie-Grant, Tahlia Anderson
Head of Editorial: Jasmin Chua
Project Editor: Antonietta Anello
Editor: Pip Thompson
Creative Director: Kristin Thomas
Designer: Celia Mance
Photographer: Nicholas Wilkins
Head of Production: Todd Rechner
Production Controller: Jessica Harvie

Colour reproduction by Splitting Image Colour Studio

Printed in China by Leo Paper Products LTD.

The paper this book is printed on is from FSC®-certified forests and other sources. FSC® promotes environmentally responsible, socially beneficial and economically viable management of the world's forests.

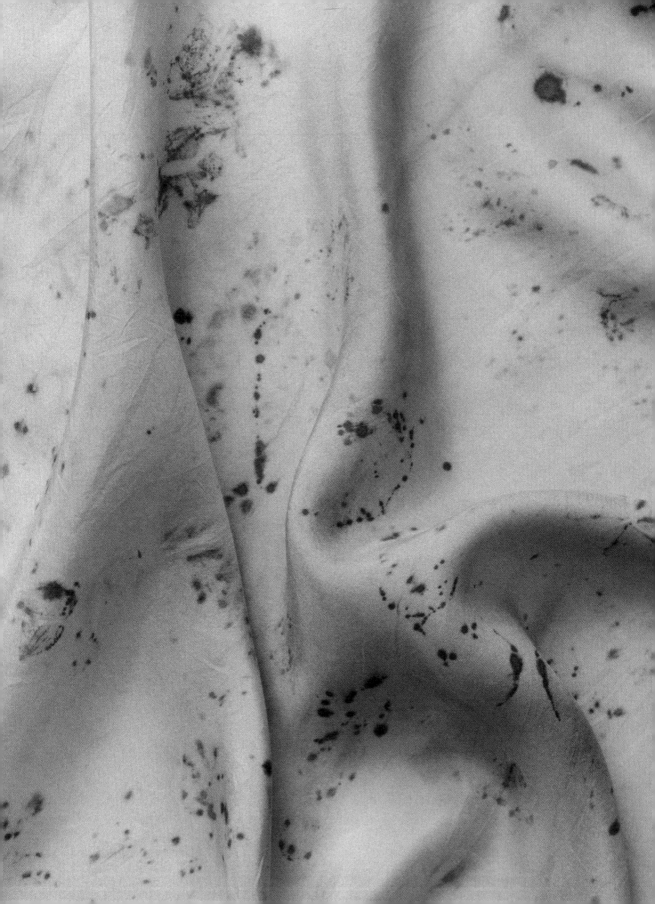